SURVIVAL SKILLS

Leading Your Church in a Changing World

STAN TOLER *and* **GLEN MARTIN**

Beacon Hill Press of Kansas City
Kansas City, Missouri

Copyright 2002
by Beacon Hill Press of Kansas City

ISBN 083-411-9188

Printed in the
United States of America

Cover Design: Michael Walsh

Library of Congress Cataloging-in-Publication Data

Toler, Stan.
    Survival skills : leading your church in a changing world / Stan Toler, Glen Martin.
        p. cm.
Includes bibliographical references.
    ISBN 0-8341-1918-8 (pbk.)
    1. Pastoral theology. I. Martin, Glen, 1953- II. Title.
    BV4011.3 .T65 2002
    253—dc21

                                                                    2002000960

10 9 8 7 6 5 4 3 2 1

To Rev. A. N. Davis,
Rev. J. Wilbur Lambert,
and Dr. Bill Burch
for friendship and pastoral wisdom
—Stan Toler

To my father, John,
and my mother, Doreen,
who gave me a passion for life,
a love of learning,
and always believed in their son
—Glen Martin

CONTENTS

ABOUT THE AUTHORS

Stan Toler is senior pastor of Trinity Church of the Nazarene in Oklahoma City and hosts the television program *Mission Today*. For the past 10 years he has taught seminars for INJOY Group, a leadership development institute. Toler has written over 45 books, including his bestsellers *God Has Never Failed Me, but He's Sure Scared Me to Death a Few Times* and *The Five-Star Church*. In his many roles of service, he finds his constant support and joy in his wife, Linda, whom he affectionately refers to as his "south Georgia peach." He shares his love for sports with their two sons, Seth Aaron and Adam James.

Glen Martin is the senior pastor of Community Baptist Church in Manhattan Beach, California. He has written and cowritten 11 other books, including *Your Pastor's Heart* and *God's Top Ten List*, both published by Moody Press. Martin speaks throughout North America on leadership, evangelism, change, and ministry effectiveness. He lives in Hermosa Beach, California, with his wife of 28 years, Nancy, and has three children: Kerry, Scott, and David.

To contact the authors
Stan Toler
P.O. Box 892170
Oklahoma City, OK 73189-2170
E-mail: stoler1107@aol.com
Web site: www.stantoler.net

Glen Martin
Community Baptist Church
1243 Artesia Boulevard
Manhattan Beach, CA 90266-6970
E-mail: glen@cbcmb.org

ACKNOWLEDGMENTS

Thank you to Deloris Leonard, Lawrence Wilson, and Pat Diamond; to Jerry Brecheisen for editorial assistance and creative merging of the authors' materials; and to Bonnie Perry, Hardy Weathers, Bruce Nuffer, and the entire team of Beacon Hill Press of Kansas City.

—Stan Toler

My heart is in the local church. Therefore, those who minister to advance the kingdom of God hold a special place in my heart. Thank you to all the pastors across North America whom I have spoken with and learned from. In particular—Sam Petitfils, you have been an immeasurable support and motivator in the ministry.

A special thanks to Conrad Lowe, now with INJOY, for his encouragement in writing this material, as well as my great teammate Stan Toler, whose love for Christ and His Church is so contagious.

—Glen Martin

1

It's All About Survival

An estimated 51 million people watched the final episode of *Survival Island*, making it one of the most watched programs in television history. Sixteen people had been "stranded" on an island near Borneo. Their plight was to eek out an existence, eating everything from bugs to rats. This summer replacement show soon became a legendary series.

Each week, viewers tuned in to see which survivor would be voted of the island by their peers. Office workers discussed the agonies and victories of the survivors around the water cooler. Soon Americans just had to know who would survive the bug bites and the backstabbing on the island.

One man survived it all to become an instant millionaire. He won because he had learned how to adapt. He won because he had taken time to understand people. He won because he had refused to be sidetracked by the pressures of the island and the personalities of the island dwellers. At last, two survivors remained in the "game" after a third survivor lost concentration during an "immunity challenge."

And then there was one. One man triumphed over the challenges and the negative votes of his fellow survivors.

Come to think of it, these episodes resembled the inner workings of some local churches! Several of the same dynamics and relational challenges are present in modern ministry (excluding the bug bites).

This book is about survival—ministry survival. These days, many pastors are worrying more about *surviving* than *succeeding.* Why? The "rules" of the game have changed. In an age of scandals, moral failures, and escalating skepticism, some even think of the Church as being on "death row."

Ministry methods that once were part of a winning arsenal are now as obsolete as a 1963 Sunday School bus. A largely godless culture has influenced the new rules of ministry. The Church of the changeless Christ is struggling to make the temporal adjustments necessary to impact that culture. Nothing seems the same. Worship, administration, service, discipleship, and fellowship don a new look to meet new demands.

I recall the story of a mother of two preschool children, one in kindergarten and the other just beginning to crawl. Suddenly Mom sensed an unnatural silence.

"Millicent, are you watching your sister?" she cried to the kindergartner.

"She's here with me," the child replied.

"Where's that?" her mother immediately inquired.

"In my room," she answered.

Mother arose quickly and ran to the child's room "Millicent, I've told you many times, you're not to carry your sister! She's much too little, and you might drop her!"

The tiny caregiver replied, "I didn't carry her, Mom."

"Well, then, how did she get to this room?"

Millicent replied proudly, "I rolled her!"

Today's ministers ponder how they arrived where they are. "New methods." But pastors are struggling not only with new methods—they're also struggling with motivation for their "game plan." They're wrestling with their perception of God's will versus their perception of a congregation's often-fickle will.

The mission, however, has not changed. This culture needs Christ. And in some cases, so does the Church. In a survey of 1,200 adults, George Barna research found that 6 out of 10 regular attendees at morning worship service say they are not born-again Christians.[1]

Ministers are uneasy at the "tribal council." Pressure? Absolutely. Theirs is a bone-weary pressure that drives some "survivors" to catch the first boat off the island. This pressure causes some team members to sit on the "beaches" of their places of service and weep over their failures. The rosters are thin enough without losing additional members of the team.

Most bookstores contain large sections designated "Pastoral Helps," "Ministry Skills," or "Leadership." Some of those sections may be better named "Wishful Thinking." Many of the helps books ooze with hope. They excite, inspire, and motivate. Some create a "bottled soda" effect. When "shaken," they generate great excitement. Then, after a glorious but decidedly brief effervescence, the fizz evaporates. What's left is as flat as a six-month-old 7-Up.

Ministers in today's culture need more than the soda effect. They need fundamental principles for putting their ideas into practice. The new millennium calls for a new ministry model. Survival in ministry demands a tough look at the issues and a game plan for the long haul.

The "Swiss Miss"

Individuals who don't recognize the need for change don't survive long. In 1968 Switzerland dominated the watch-making world. Swiss craftsmen led as undisputed leaders for three prior decades, and there was no doubt that they would lead for decades to come. "Buy a Swiss watch" was good advice for anybody shopping for a watch in the 1960s and 1970s.

Building top-quality watches was not the only Swiss specialty. They were also innovators in timekeeping. They invented the minute and second hands. Teams of Swiss researchers developed better gears and mainsprings. No one waterproofed a watch like the Swiss. Their dominance was unquestioned. They captured 65 percent of the watch market and more than 90 percent of watch-making profits—until 1980.

In 1980 the rules changed. The market shifted, and *the Swiss missed it.* Watchmakers entered the electronic age. The finely crafted Swiss gears, bearings, and mainsprings became irrelevant as electronics replaced the mechanical technology of watchmaking. Financial catastrophe ensued as five-sixths of all Swiss watchmakers lost their jobs. Japan, on the other hand, flourished and captured 33 percent of the market in two years.

Incredibly, the Swiss could have avoided this problem. They invented the electronic quartz movement, but in 1967 they rejected this revolutionary innovation. This thinking did not fit their paradigm, and they refused to make a shift. They didn't survive.

The Swiss watchmakers aren't the only ones who have missed it. Nations that did not adjust to changing times have sunk into oblivion. Once-flourishing organizations have lost their impact because they failed to *rethink* and *retool.* The Church is not immune to such misses.

In his book *The Death of the Church,* Mike Regele draws a razor-sharp parallel:

> The institutional church in America finds itself in the same place. It has built up many structures of self-dependence upon which it relies and into which it pours great resources. Yet these structures are failing . . . What are the options? Simply, we can die because of our hidebound resistance to change, or we can die in order to live. As an institution, the American church must choose between these two. There are no other options. However, it is not as easy as merely examining the two options and choosing. The reality is that the church is already on a direct course toward the first option.[2]

The purpose of this book is to help pastors avoid the "Swiss miss" of the watchmakers. How? First, by helping them to anticipate the future, to look at both the trends and the times. Second, by helping them learn the survival skills necessary for ministry in the new millennium.

The Changing Face of the Church

The following E-mail message from an unknown source is a poignant reminder of change in North American culture:

The people who are starting college this fall were born in the early 80s. They have no meaningful recollection of the Reagan era, and many don't even know that he was shot in an attempted assassination. They were preteens when the Persian Gulf War was waged. Black Monday, 1987, is no more significant to them than the Great Depression. There was only been one pope during their lifetime. They clearly remember only one president. They were 11 years old when the Soviet Union broke apart and do not remember the Cold War. They have never feared a nuclear war.

The *Day After* is a pill to them, not a movie, and *CCCP* is just a bunch of letters, not a reference to Soviet Russia. They have known only one Germany. They don't remember the explosion of the space shuttle *Challenger* or the massacre at Tienamen Square. They don't know who Mu'ammar Gadhafi is. Their lifetime has always included the threat of AIDS. To them, bottle caps have not only always been screwed off, but have always been plastic.

Atari predates them, as do vinyl record albums. The expression "You sound like a broken record" means nothing to them. They have never owned a record player. They have likely never played Pac Man and have never heard of *Pong*. The special effects in *Star Wars* look fake to them. To them there have always been blue M & Ms, and they've never seen the beige ones. The compact disc was introduced before they were 3 years old. As far as they know, stamps never cost less than 33 cents. They don't remember the five-digit ZIP code and have always had an answering machine.

Analog methods will not impact this digital age. Ministry survivors will have to adapt to reach the cell phone citizens of this era who have no church history.

The Changing Face of Ministry

In *The Issachar Factor,* Gary McIntosh and Glen Martin propose that everyone must become "sons of Issachar." 1 Chron. 12:32 notes that these men "understood the times and knew what [to] do." The writers polled many pastors who made the transition from ministry in the 1950s to ministry in the 1990s and asked them to record the changes. Responses provided enough data to write an entire book! Most pastors indicated their role had changed significantly. Let's examine that changing role of ministry in this new millennium.

First, we need to compare the contemporary ministry model with the previous one. From the 1950s through the 1990s, a typical pastor's job description included three items:

1. The pastor *served as the protector of the truth.* People interested in the church's position on issues such as the Rapture, the Atonement, or the Trinity asked the pastor. The pastor protected the doctrines of the church like a pit bull.

2. The pastor *assisted believers through life transitions.* When a young couple desired to get married, they sought counsel from their pastor. When that couple had a baby, the pastor presided over the parent's dedication of the little one to God before the witnessing congregation. When the child came to saving faith in Christ, the pastor administered the sacrament of baptism. When a family member died, the pastor officiated the funeral. The pastor was everywhere!

3. The pastor *served as primary caregiver and the primary evangelist* in the church. When parishioners headed to the hospital, the pastor visited. When newcomers appeared in church, the pastor visited their home and led their assimilation into the life of the faith community.

In some ways pastors still fulfill these expectations,

even in the new millennium. In today's world, however, the church has added new expectations:

1. The pastor must be a *leader* and a *mentor.*

2. The pastor must be the *facilitator* of pastoral care rather than the primary caregiver. Though they must not abandon personal pastoral care, wise pastors find ways to include trained lay ministers in the pastoral care of the congregation.

3. The pastor must be a *missiologist.* Neighborhoods are changing. Our nation is more ethnically complex. The postmodern worldview presents new challenges.

Pastors are scrambling for help in understanding their roles. If "carrying" no longer works, then "rolling" must be implemented!

Looking Forward, Looking Back

Like an automobile, most churches are equipped with a "rearview mirror." They often spend more time looking at where they came from rather than where they're going. Some churches have such a huge rearview mirror that the leaders can't see out the windshield! Ministry survival skills help us learn how to reduce the size of the rearview mirror (without necessarily removing it) so the congregation can look through the windshield.

Richard accepted the call to pastor a church in a major city. The sanctuary platform of the church was furnished with four large chairs—ministry "thrones." After a year of ministry, Richard noticed that only he and his worship leader sat on the platform. Two of the chairs were unused every Sunday. Pastor Richard decided to remove the two unused chairs and replace them with greenery to enhance the décor.

Unwittingly, Richard had just poked a stick into a hornet's nest!

An anonymous letter explained the conflict. "You can't remove those two chairs," the writer explained. "Dr. _____ [a well-known television pastor] has four chairs on his platform."

Little did Pastor Richard know that those four "ministry thrones" on his platform once graced the platform of that television pastor. The removal of the chairs constituted a shift in orthodoxy and bordered on anarchy!

Pastor Richard needed to learn some ministry survival skills. He needed to learn how to minimize the rear view and maximize the forward view.

How important it is to keep an eye on the horizon in these changing times! Ponder some of the fundamental changes in recent years in our culture:

Environmentalism is now a worldview.

Terrorism is an everyday activity.

Leadership is no longer respected.

Cursing and sexual scenes are normal television fare.

Satellite communications and cellular phones are commonplace.

Many homes are wired for access to the Internet.

Alternative lifestyles are routinely accepted.

"Safe sex," rather than abstinence, is routinely taught in public schools.

Fad diets have replaced "three square meals."

New Age philosophies have become enormously popular.

Biotechnological advancements have created new ethical dilemmas.

The Church must not be caught staring in the rearview mirror while this New World Order screams by. New skills are necessary for new times. Leaders must be confident in God's strength and provision. Where He leads, He provides.

The Church of the 21st century is on a journey of preparation. Leaders must first prepare their hearts and immerse themselves in God's vision for their ministry. Then through their praying, preparation, organization, and vision casting, every age and stage of life in the Church will catch the God-granted enthusiasm. Ministry infused with divine life will be the result.

The human tendency is to procrastinate appropriate action. Unfinished symphonies, half-written books, uncompleted canvases, and incomplete buildings are all around us. However, God completes His work. Did you ever see a sunset and remark, "That is only half a sunset?" Did you ever see a seascape and ask, "Why did God not complete the sea?" Phil. 1:6 reminds every leader on Survivor Island, "Being confident of this, that he who began a good work in you will carry it on to completion until the day of Christ Jesus."

The Changing Impact of the Church

The Church's impact on society has drastically changed. Those changes are viewed in three stages:

1. Anticipation

Fifty years ago church leaders anticipated change by observing the youth culture. George Hunter described a youth culture "with its own distinct (and evolving) norms for clothing and hairstyles, with its own jargon and dance and music."[3]

In the early 1960s, church attendance began declining. Society experienced tremendous social and economic upheavals, while the Church maintained status quo. Church leaders feared change. But in that era, God did some miraculous things outside organized churches. Parachurch organizations, such as Campus Crusade for Christ, began growing and assuming ministry for the struggling church.

2. Innovation

By the mid-1960s, the Christian community had shifted some paradigms and had made some radical adjustments. Donald McGavran's new emphasis on church growth purported that change was necessary if the Church was to grow. Win Arn, C. Peter Wagner, and Elmer Towns traveled the country, training pastors to open the front door and close the back door of the Church. Books poured from printing presses as pastors began searching for new manuals on statistical analysis and new methodologies for greater effectiveness.

The Church entered the electronic age. Through the 1970s and 1980s, "seeker-sensitivity" emerged, and new worship forms gained acceptance. Music changed, seating arrangements changed, sermons changed, and many churches changed. Tradition no longer ruled. Thankfully, the Church continued its commitment to the Bible. But a new vision arose to involve the entire Body of Christ in its mission, using all of its gifts and talents.

3. Excellence

The stage of excellence began in the mid-to-late 1990s, when the Church recognized it had become complacent, using the methods of previous decades. Pastors began to clamor for new ideas.

Megachurch pastors like Bill Hybels and Rick Warren modeled church growth and innovative techniques. Cutting-edge books like Stan Toler's and Alan Nelson's *The Five-Star Church* called for excellence and urged the readers to develop skills to advance the local church.[4]

The decade ended with a mass "Y2K" phobia concerning predicted computer meltdowns and the end of the world. As the Church looked to the future millennium, some of its members doubted they would see it. A sobering gray cloud hung over the Church.

New Year's Day 2000 arrived, bringing a collective smile and sign of relief. The last night of 1999 had ended without a calamity. But what next? First, many members wondered what they would do with all that Y2K surplus! Then they looked squarely at the beckoning call of ministry reality.

Where do we go from here?

Decline or Change?

With the dawning of the new millennium, church leaders continued wrestling with some challenges begun in the prior decade. Some leaders refused to embrace new methods and new ministries. Some engaged "the battle of the bulletin" as the "worship wars" escalated. Some churches divided over the new versus the old ways. Some pastors anchored one foot in the past and held on to their congregations as they attempted to move forward.

The refusal to change resulted in a lack of direction in many churches. Consider the following illustration. While pastoring in Kelowna, British Columbia, and serving as a volunteer for the Royal Canadian Mounted Police, Tim Schroeder responded to an accident call one night. A long stretch of road ended with a 90-degree turn. Beyond the curve was a swamp. The spot was a favorite for local drag racers, and there had been a number of bad accidents as the young drivers had failed to make the turn. Fearing the worst, Tim hurried to the scene to find a car off the end of the road. It had flown into the air and landed in the swamp.

Tim waded through the water and discovered an elderly couple still in the car. No one was seriously injured, but the lady was shaken. Tim and his partner carried the woman to an ambulance and helped her husband to the police car. Tim asked the gentleman what had caused the accident. With disgust, he replied, "Oh, I just got these new eye glasses today and, to tell you the truth, I couldn't tell whether I was looking through my bifocal or my trifocal! I didn't see the corner, so I just kept going the way I was!"

This man's predicament may bring a chuckle. But how often does this scenario parallel life in the Church? If at this intersection in history church leaders don't develop new skills for new times, seek to understand the changing environment, and negotiate the turns, the Church will keep going the way it's been going. If leaders are stubborn enough, they may journey a long way in this millennium before realizing that the road turned and that some of their followers went the other way.

This does not need to happen. The remainder of this book is designed to help church leaders discover ministry skills for the new era. By taking the initiative to adapt, adjust, and change, leaders can effectively help their churches impact their culture for Christ in these fragile days.

Important Survival Choices

Every reader will be confronted with three basic choices in the pages that follow:

- Maintain the present way of ministry and refuse change.
- Adjust the present way of ministry and accept change.
- Change the present way of ministry and influence change.

Regrettably, the first choice will be the most common over the next 10 years. But those who choose the last two will see growth and consequently will need survival skills. This book is designed as a guide for making adjustments in leadership and ministry style to influence positive change.

I challenge church leaders to learn these skills with a heart for God and a hand for others in need. The call of God is compelling, and the providential supply of God is available for the claiming.

The Golden Gate Bridge was built between 1933 and 1937. During the first half of construction, over a dozen men fell off the superstructure, plunging 700 feet to their death. Joseph Strauss, director of the project, stopped construction and ordered a giant safety net anchored under the site. During the second half of construction, about half a dozen fell, but their lives were spared. After the net was placed, work proceeded at 25 percent greater efficiency! Knowing the net was there infused confidence in the workmen and inspired efficiency.

Christian leaders may stumble and fall, may become fearful and frustrated. But there's a net underneath called God's grace. He catches His workers, forgives them, and re-establishes them. Heb. 10:19-23 says,

> Therefore, brothers, since we have confidence to enter the Most Holy Place by the blood of Jesus, by a new

and living way opened for us through the curtain, that is, his body, and since we have a great priest over the house of God, let us draw near to God with a sincere heart in full assurance of faith, having our hearts sprinkled to cleanse us from a guilty conscience and having our bodies washed with pure water. Let us hold unswervingly to the hope we profess, for he who promised is faithful.

How wonderful the day when every leader can say, "My sins are forgiven, my eternity is assured, my present is empowered, and 'I can do all things through Christ who strengthens me'" (Phil. 4:13, NKJV).

2

VISION SKILLS

ON A FLIGHT TO CHICAGO, the pilot announced that the takeoff had been postponed due to mechanical failure.

Later the flight attendant made another announcement. Everyone who was heading for Chicago was to remain on the plane. Forgetting the intercom was still on, the pilot was heard to utter, "Whoops!"

Soon he was heading down the aisle of the plane to the back exit ramp, with hat in hand and briefcase in tow.

"Where do you think you're going?" a brazen passenger asked the pilot.

He whispered, "Denver."

The passenger replied, "This plane's not going to Denver—it's going to Chicago!"

"I know," the embarrassed pilot answered. "I'm on the wrong plane!"

One of the most important ministry skills for this new millennium is the ability to head the organization in the right direction, to project a purpose and a plan for the future, to cast a vision.

Vision is commonly understood to be the act or power of anticipating what will or may come to be. That definition tells only part of the story. Some folks can imagine the future in all its brilliance. But for a vision to have impact, it must have the power to motivate people and shape events. That is to say, vision must have the power to move people

- as a team
- in a set direction
- over a prolonged period of time
- toward a distant goal

That goal must be worthy of hard work, perseverance, and sacrifice. The life of Abraham Lincoln demonstrates the power of that kind of vision. At an important turning point in the Civil War,

Union General George Meade had just won a great victory over Robert E. Lee at the Battle of Gettysburg. But as Lee was beating a retreat, Meade was slow in his pursuit. As a result, Lee escaped back to Virginia with much of his army intact. When Meade boasted of his success in "driving every vestige of the invader from our soil," Lincoln was not at all pleased. He was infuriated.

"Drive the invader from our soil!" he cried. "Will our generals never get the idea: The whole country is our soil."

Lincoln had a vision. To him, it was a mighty compass —guiding his action through every crisis and through every twist and turn in the war. At the center of his vision was the idea of one country—whole and indivisible. From the inception of the conflict, Lincoln never wavered in his commitment to the idea that the United States must endure as one country, dedicated—in his words—to the proposition of "government of the people, by the people and for the people."[1]

The Church has also been given a vision. Like Lincoln's, it directs God's people as a compass towards a preferable future. But this happens only in the church that remains true to its calling and true to its Captain, the Lord Jesus Christ.

Terminology Confusion

As new terminology has invaded the Church, some have expressed confusion over the meaning of certain words. One pastor recently said, "I have a mission—or is it a vision—or are they goals? Oh, who cares? God will sort it all out!" We care. Those who follow us will struggle to know where we're going if our terms sound confusing. Here's an overview of the terms associated with vision casting.

Mission. Our *mission* is the statement that never changes. It's spelled out for us in the Word of God. The mission is the big picture that has already been defined by Scripture and offers the answer to the question "Why do we exist?"

"It is very likely that many churches share the same mission and could even use the same wording of that mission."[2] You may be familiar with the Shorter Westminster Confession, which asks and answers the question on mission, "What is the chief end of man? To glorify God and enjoy Him forever."

Vision. The *vision* of a church is unique to the personality and passion of that local assembly of believers. It provides focus and details about the future. The vision of the church is what God has called a Body of Believers to accomplish for His kingdom. The vision is inspiring, exciting, and it challenges the people toward a preferable future.

Your church may declare, "Our vision is to reach every home in this community with the gospel of Jesus Christ." If so, then that should be the focus of each of its ministries. It should be the centerpiece of its programming. That is the vision of the church.

Values. *Values* are the nonnegotiable characteristics of a local ministry. They guide and enable leaders to say a word in the ministry not heard very often: *no.* If a new ministry is proposed, it must immediately be run through the grid of values to determine whether it will make a viable contribution to the church's endeavor. If it will, then the ministry is moved to the next level of planning and strategizing. If the newly developed program does not meet the criteria of the values of the church, then it faces the big "NO!"

Goals. *Goals* represent what the church desires to accomplish within a certain time frame. For example, some pastors include a "Vision Sunday" in their calendar. Prayerfully and carefully, a goal—regarding property, ministry, attendance, or finances—is presented to the congregation with great enthusiasm. The distinct purpose of the presentation is to motivate the people to a collective reaching of the announced goal.

These are the objective criteria for measuring effectiveness and determining the appropriation of personnel and resources. Goals are manifested in the local church ministry in a variety of areas.

Strategy. *Strategy* goes hand in hand with goals. Strategy is the plan for accomplishing the vision. It incorporates all the other facets in a way that provides the most efficient means of getting the job done.

The Importance of Vision Skills

Why are vision skills so important for pastoring in this new century and millennium? *Vision* is paramount for accomplishing the stated *mission*. Notice the diagram below. The grid identifies leadership results that result from two factors: the focus of the vision, and the teamwork of the people.

Focused Vision

Fragmentation	*Oneness/Direction*

Individual ← → **Team-Oriented**

Stagnation/Decline	*Frustration*

Unfocused Vision

Let's examine the four quadrants. If the vision is highly focused, the people develop a team orientation. The result is unity in direction.

On that first *Survivor Island* episode, some of the island inhabitants were seen forming an alliance. Their purpose wasn't very righteous, however. It was to get someone outside their inner group voted off the island.

Conversely, a positive alliance can be seen in the example of the wall-builders in the eighth chapter of Nehemiah. The walls were up in just 52 days, an incredible accomplishment. Most of us couldn't get the required building permits in that amount of time! Those who have seen these walls in Jerusalem firsthand know how monumental that task really was. The people had a common commitment, a "oneness" in direction. They developed an alliance built around Nehemiah's vision.

If there had not been a clearly focused vision, the result would have been far different. What if the leadership had not come to an agreement on the need to build the walls? The result would have been mass *confusion* instead of massive construction. When the people are willing to move and build (or minister), the leaders must know where they want to lead them.

Hindrances to Vision

The other side of the vision grid deals with the selfishness of the people. The vision may be clear and the leaders may have done their utmost to present the vision with focus. Yet if the people have their own agenda—their own individual expectations—there will be fragmentation. "Trivial Pursuit" will no longer be just a game. It will become the lifestyle of the people as arguments ensue over such trivial matters as color choices and room allocations. The people will be polarized over issues that have little or nothing to do with the mission of the church.

The final quadrant demonstrates what happens when

the people are selfish and the vision is unfocused. The result is stagnation and decline. This is where the vast majority of churches in North America are languishing. The people are unrestrained. They have an "I" problem.

"This is what *I* want."

"This is what *I* expect."

"If you want my money, this is the way *I* want things!"

Here's another way of understanding this phenomenon.

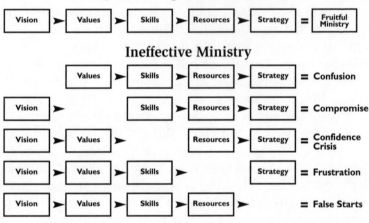

Effective ministry takes place when
- Vision is in place.
- Values provide parameters for planning.
- Leaders and people are skilled for the task.
- Resources have been provided.
- Strategy is in effect.

But what if one of these governing qualities is missing? The absence of vision creates confusion. This truth is certainly given in Scripture: "Where there is no revelation [vision], the people cast off restraint" (Prov. 29:18).

In the absence of values, the church will find that leaders compromise easily. Ministries are established and kept on life support for decades, even though they're not accomplishing the vision.

The absence of vision skill development will result in an atmosphere in which people lose their confidence. They want to become active contributors to the cause but are afraid of failure and disappointment.

Resources and Vision

The elimination of resources leads to frustration. People buy into the vision and align themselves with the values. They're ready to go, but the budget is struggling. There are no resources to move ahead.

The absence of strategy generates false starts. The church may try a ministry or program, but when it fails, the idea is placed on the shelf. It may have been a great idea at the time, such as small group ministries, for example. Then, five years down the road, a new leader discovers— you guessed it—small groups. Another attempt to launch this ministry will probably meet with the same action: shelved once more.

Most of us have gone through each of these cycles at some point. That's why the driving factor for effective ministry is *vision*.

So the first survival skill that must be mastered by the effective leader is vision skill: the ability to establish a powerful vision and then cast that vision in such a way that people are compelled to be a part of the team, remaining focused on the "preferable future."

The following are the essential characteristics of an effective vision.

The Qualities of an Effective Vision

Many years ago Charlton Heston was interviewed on the *Merv Griffin Show.* This was at a time in Mr. Heston's life and career when he had gained much attention from his two megamovies, *The Ten Commandments* and *Ben Hur*. In this interview, Griffin asked a question that many of us had wanted to ask this big star of the religious screen: "Has your spiritual outlook changed any because of these two movies?"

Heston thought for a moment and then said, "Well, Merv, you can't walk barefoot down Mount Sinai and be the same person you were when you went up."

Good answer. Why was Moses different when he descended Mount Sinai? He was captured by the vision of the glory of God. Vision has a way of doing that. Peter saw the miracle of the Lord providing a bounty of fish, and he left his nets to follow Christ. Paul caught a vision of our risen Lord and left his former life of persecution in order to follow Jesus.

Throughout history, men and women have laid aside everything dear to them to follow the vision Christ has put into their hearts, a vision to make a difference in the world. What qualities make a vision so compelling that people are motivated by it and the Kingdom is built because of it?

1. Vision must be rooted in God's will.

The first quality of an effective vision for God's people is that it must be based on what they believe God wants them to do. God's will isn't some extraterrestrial hide-and-seek. God wants you to know His plan. Our Lord delights in unmasking what was once thought to be the "mystery of His will" for the Church. Search the Scriptures. The mission of the Church is clear. We call it the Great Commission. Spend time alone with that vision, dreaming, praying, seeking His guidance for utilizing it in the ministry He has entrusted to you.

2. Vision motivates people to action.

Effective vision motivates people to leave their comfort zone. Let's face it: leaders and people can get lazy. Many would opt for a "remote control" ministry that would allow them to remain in the lounge chair of the family room instead of riding a warhorse toward the battlefield. Everyone needs to be moved to attempt great things. It should break our hearts to see what God sees—lonely, lost people in search of truth. Likewise, it should challenge our hearts to realize that he wants us to be a part of the plan to reach those people.

3. Vision paints a picture of the future.

Vision appeals simultaneously to logic and feeling. A vision generates feelings of hope for a future accomplishment. Jesus gathered His disciples around Him and pointed to people coming toward Him. "Look at the fields" (John 4:35). He was saying, "Look at the possibilities for bringing hope to the hopeless!"

4. Vision generates enthusiasm and openness to change.

Vision always produces change. For example, accepting God's vision in a person's life is a process of spiritual change we call sanctification. God may love us just the way we are, but He loves us too much to have us stay that way! "Vision is initiated by God, is desired by his people and is conveyed through the Holy Spirit. God communicates his vision only to those who have persisted in knowing him intimately, for his vision is a sacred part of unfolding his eternal plan."[3] A ministry vision prompts people to desire what God desires—bringing the message of hope to the hopeless.

5. Vision must be practical.

Vision is both achievable and believable. The end result may not come according to our timing. Only God can determine when we're ready to handle it. But when casting vision to followers, the leader must make sure they can *see* the desired result and believe it can be accomplished in God's time.

6. Vision must be clear enough to guide decision making.

Vision gives an organization the ability to say, "No" to activities that won't contribute to the cause. George Barna writes, "Vision is tangible to the beholder. Although it is just a concept or perspective of a nonexistent reality, vision exists within the mind of a visionary so clearly that it may be thought of as a living image. Such a vision motivates and directs ministry, filters information, serves as a catalyst in decision making and measures progress."[4]

7. Vision focuses resources in a common direction.

Ministering in a postmodern world is not easy. At one time the rules for pastoring and leading a church were well defined and the boundaries clearly marked. But in this new millennium everything is different. Using a basketball analogy, it's as if we're playing basketball but the rules have changed midseason. Let's imagine that we've studied all the past strategies for winning a basketball championship. And let's say that we've been given a coaching position at a prestigious university. But suddenly we're confronted with the following new rules:

- A player may dribble the ball only three times before passing.
- A player is allowed only five seconds in the lane.
- Shots made while the player is blindfolded earn five points.
- Only guards (usually the shortest players) can rebound.
- Opposing coaches can eject one player from the other team at halftime.

I think we'd all say, "Wait a minute! I wasn't trained to coach with these rules!" Those same words may be expressed by pastors in this new century and millennium. The rules have changed. Ministry no longer takes place "inside the box." The box has been either redefined or removed.

8. Vision will outlive the visionary.

If a vision is truly from the Lord, it won't fade if the "vision-caster" is taken home to be with the Lord or moves on to another ministry. The apostle Paul's vision was clear and distinct: "It has always been my ambition to preach the gospel where Christ was not known, so that I would not be building on someone else's foundation" (Rom. 15:20).

Paul planted numerous churches in keeping with the vision he was given. He was creative and became known as a risktaker. He remarked, "Though I am free and belong to no man, I make myself a slave to everyone, to win as many as possible. To the Jews I became like a Jew, to win the Jews. To those under the law I became like one under the law (though I myself am not under the law), so as to win those under the law. To those not having the law I became like one not having the law (though I am not free from God's law but am under Christ's law), so as to win those not having the law" (1 Cor. 9:19-21).

These strategies broke new ground in evangelism. But the vision didn't end with Paul's demise. His evangelistic spirit permeates many churches today.

Steps to Casting a Great Vision

A vision will affect no one if it is not communicated. Buckminster Fuller, inventor of the geodesic dome, captured the essence of vision casting and the sense of urgency behind it when he said, "The world's term paper is due. We've done enough research and read enough books. We've studied for centuries. Now it's time to write. God wants the paper turned in now."[5] This is not the time for the Church to sit back and watch. We're in a tremendous time of transition that demands the following aggressive steps in casting a great vision:

1. **Create a leadership team.** Effective leaders have an agenda. They're not afraid to individually take charge, dream dreams, and move toward a focused goal. Today's complex needs, however, call for teaming in ministry. This model provides a more stable architecture for the future of the church than individual effort. An effective church lead-

ership team includes both forward thinkers and those who have learned from the church's past.

Leaders seek out key lay leaders they believe will greatly influence the church. As primary leader, the pastor must not only be on this team but also be willing to direct it. This responsibility cannot be passed on to others. The leadership team will not so much be initiating change as establishing direction.

The pastor will want to recruit people who know how to lead others, have a sense of discernment, and are committed to prayer. These spiritual direction-setters will serve as a balance to the visionaries.

A leadership team will be cognizant of the history of leaders and the church. Every leader has a history, a series of events through which God leads in the maturing process. The church also has a history. Every local congregation, except for a newly planted one, was established on the dreams of another group of people. With that history come enduring themes that create continuity and stability. Soliciting *buy-in* from the leadership team validates wholesome respect for the church's past and allows building for the future.

2. Agree on a process. The process of vision writing and vision casting is as delicate as putting eyeliner on a caterpillar. While it is time-consuming, it is also very rewarding. Jim Garlow, pastor of San Diego's Skyline Wesleyan Church, continually warns his staff not to "minister for the moment." He says, "There is no success without sacrifice. If I succeed without sacrifice, then it's because someone who went before me made the sacrifice. If I sacrifice and don't see success, then someone who follows will reap success from my sacrifice." Probably the finest biblical example of this investment principle is found in the "heroes of faith" chapter of the Book of Hebrews. The writer says, "All these people were still living by faith when they died. They did not receive the things promised; they only saw them and welcomed them from a distance. And they admitted that they were aliens and strangers on earth" (11:13).

When the process begins, each member of the team must agree that he or she is doing business for *eternity*. The details of that eternity mission include a commitment to follow through when assignments are issued. A target must be established.

"Where are we aiming?"

"What will the end product look like?"

"Will we accept the time commitment required to see this vital work to completion?"

"How will we work as a team to accomplish this?"

Anything less than a unified effort will limit the process.

3. Get the facts. Every church has its own culture. Before establishing a new direction, a leader must recognize all factors that have contributed to the church's functioning. Bert Nanus once said, "Legends, tradition, and habits tend to persist for a long time and determine the organizational culture—that is, 'how we do things around here.' Past visions often continue to influence present behaviors and may have a certain nostalgic attraction that makes them difficult to dislodge."[6]

One way to obtain the facts is to identify the "sacred cows" of the church. Every church has them, and they typically fall into five categories:

The unwritten cows are church preferences that rarely surface until an agent for change proposes an alteration. For instance, on Fred's first Sunday in his new pastorate, he sat on the front pew discussing the order of service with his youth pastor. Soon he received a tap on the shoulder by a long-time member who reminded him that he shouldn't be talking while the organ is playing.

"Young man, you should be getting your heart ready for worship."

Fred said later, "I didn't know this was a rule. No one shared this detail with me during the candidacy process. It was a rule etched in the minds of everyone but me." In other words, he had just had an encounter with an *unwritten cow*.

The written cows are the bylaws and policy manuals. These written rules and regulations govern the operation of the church and are often treated as they were as sacred as the Decalogue! Try breaking one of these written commandments, and you'll find yourself a candidate for a "sanctified stoning."

The turf cows emerge when competing personalities vie for position, influence, or power. Ongoing arguments between the children's programs, children's Sunday School activities, and day school are examples of these "border wars." It's not unusual to see a corporate ruffling of the feathers when, for instance, there are only *two* bulletin boards for *three* ministries.

The denominational cows are rules and regulations sent from the top down. They have a wider impact than the "written cows" of the local church. In some instances, when "denominational cows" are ignored, the pastor could suddenly find himself or herself put out to pasture!

The personal cows are the personal likes and dislikes of the congregation. One group likes one style of music while another group prefers something else. One group enjoys a certain style of teaching or preaching while another group wants the opposite. One group like noise while the other likes solitude. It's like the church usher greeting parishioners at the entrance to the sanctuary with seating options: "Will that be clapping or no clapping?"

Smart leaders gain as many facts as possible before initiating the vision-casting process. They examine trends affecting the people in the church. As they think ahead for needed adjustments, they research the current stage in the life cycle of the church. And they'll also be aware of the current life stages of the people.

4. Determine the church's readiness for change. Not every church is ready for change, even though it may be necessary. A forward-looking leader will take the vital signs of the congregation. What are the signs that the people are willing to invest time and energy for change?

First, you'll find positive faith. The church is filled with people who anticipate something great happening every week. They come to church with a sense of expectation, looking for God's hand to move.

Second, the people have confidence in their leaders. There are no surprises. The leaders have made wise decisions in the past and have communicated well to the people.

Third, the church has experienced some previous success. Every leader needs a few "belt notches" before tackling another major hurdle. A good leader knows the benefit of preparing for a big victory with smaller wins.

Fourth, the church budget is healthy. Vision requires funding. Plans are nice, but "money talks." Say, "Show me the money," and you'll learn something about the priorities of the church!

Finally, the staff is established. Advancing a vision immediately after a significant staff changeover is not wise. The church often goes into shock after such a major change and may require a period of recuperation. The church with a stable leadership is better poised to cast a vision.

5. Decide on the core values. Remember that values are not the same as doctrinal statements and bylaws. And values are not the *vision* of the church. Values guide the church. Values take diverse people and harness them together in a positive direction. Values become the grid by which plans are made. Values should be universally applied to all ministries. They are practical. They are repeatable. And they must be biblical.

For example, the core values of Community Baptist Church, where Glen Martin pastors, provide a splendid example of how a church can incorporate values into its mission statement. Notice that the statement is broken into sections with bold letters, while the eight core values uphold and support them.

COMMUNITY BAPTIST CHURCH

OUR MISSION STATEMENT

**As a community of worshipers,
we have been sent into the world . . .**

OUR CORE VALUES

❶ *Celebrating Jesus Christ.* We believe that passion for the Lord should undergird everything we do, for we are, first and foremost, a community of worshipers (Phil. 4:4; 3:7-11; Matt. 22:36-40; 1 Pet. 2:9; John 4:23).

❷ *Leading with integrity.* We believe that our leaders must be "full of the Spirit and wisdom" (Acts 6:3) if our church is to faithfully carry out its mission to the world (Heb. 13:7, 17; 1 Pet. 5:2-3; Acts 20:28; 1 Tim. 4:15-16).

to make disciples (Growing in numbers)

❸ *Balancing our commitments.* We believe that effective disciple-making requires a balance of biblical faithfulness, cultural relevance, and total dependence upon God (Acts 14:21-23; John 8:31; 1 Cor. 9:19-23; Prov. 3:5-6).

❹ *Targeting the unchurched.* We believe that lost people matter to God, and so we do everything we can to reach them with the good news about Jesus Christ (Luke 5:30-32; 15; 19:10; John 3:16-17; 1 Tim. 2:3-4; 2 Pet. 3:9).

to mature disciples (Growing in depth)

❺ *Renewing our minds.* We believe that people are transformed by understanding and applying God's Word, and so we encourage and provide for biblical learning (Rom. 12:2; Eph. 4:22-24; 2 Tim. 3:16-17; 4:1-5).

❻ *Connecting with others.* We believe that disciples can grow only in a context of loving relationships, and so we urge everyone to be active in a smaller group (Acts 2:42-47; Heb. 10:24-25; John 13:34-35; Gal. 6:2).

and to mobilize disciples (Growing in ministry)

❼ *Equipping for service.* We believe that every disciple is gifted to serve others in love, and so we encourage and train people for compassionate service (Eph. 4:11-16; 1 Pet. 4:10; Rom. 12:4-8; Gal. 6:9-10).

❽ *Sharing our faith.* We believe that every disciple is empowered to share Jesus Christ with others, and so we encourage and train people for bold witness (Acts 1:8; Acts 8:1, 4; 2 Cor. 2:14; 5:17-21; Matt. 5:16; 1 Thess. 1:7-8).

who love the Lord our God above all else and who touch others with the reality of Jesus Christ.

6. Write out the vision. This may be one of the most important responsibilities undertaken by a leader. Take it seriously. Spend hours in prayer with the leadership team as they anticipate the writing of a vision. Get away for a retreat. Undertake a series of workshops, gaining input from ministry heads in the church. Collect vision statements from other churches—those ahead of yours in their journey.

Most important, stay united. This is no simple task. Paul wrote about it: "Make every effort to keep the unity of the Spirit through the bond of peace" (Eph. 4:3). In other words, unity will take time and work. Keep the leadership team committed to learning together, creating the vision together, and supporting one another at all costs.

At his INJOY Conferences, John Maxwell offers six suggestions for receiving and writing a vision statement:
- Look within you—What do you feel?
- Look behind you—What have I learned?
- Look around you—What is happening in other churches?
- Look ahead of you—What do I want to accomplish?
- Look above you—What part does God play?
- Look beside you—What resources are available to you?[7]

Here are three additional hints. *First, make the vision statement brief.* Brevity is beautiful! Keep your vision statement to about 25-30 words. *Second, use terminology that can be understood by everyone.* Use terms that even the unchurched will understand. *Third, stay focused on what the church "must" do.* A well-written vision becomes the foundation for building appropriate strategy and goals.

7. Gain "buy-in" from the remainder of the leadership. What would it have been like to be among the crowd following the Lord when He fed the 5,000 as recorded in John 6? Wherever Jesus ministered, He drew a crowd. The vast majority of these people were merely curious. "What will Jesus do next?" "I wonder if He'll do another miracle before we have to go home!" The Lord was interested in moving the crowd from curiosity to commitment.

After feeding the 5,000, our Lord turned to these folks and asked them, "Did you enjoy the food? Aren't you glad you were here today? You all realize this bread you have eaten is the basic food of the Jewish people, but I want to tell you—I am the bread that came down from heaven."

Hold everything!

The challenge was felt immediately as John records, "On hearing it, many of his disciples said, 'This is a hard teaching. Who can accept it?'" (John 6:60). The multitude of the curious would not buy into Christ's vision—that God's hand was upon His life. But those who moved from curiosity to commitment immediately bought into Christ's vision.

Remember: very few people are motivated without being pushed.

8. Communicate the vision. The leader's primary task during vision casting and change is persuasion—he or she must persuade the people of both the importance of the vision and the timing of the vision. This task presents both the greatest opportunity and the greatest challenge for a leader who is seeking to transform a church ministry. That leader must effectively communicate

- The *need* for a new vision for the health of the church.
- The *rightness* of the vision for the people in the body.
- The leader's *commitment* to fulfilling the vision.
- The *benefits* of following the vision.
- The *impact* for the kingdom of God through the vision.

Vision-casting skill requires constantly reminding the people of these things. Preach a sermon series, hang banners, pass out bookmarks, present case studies of where the vision is making a difference. Establish prayer teams who will pray a covering over the fulfillment of God's vision. Whatever it takes, keep the vision before the people.

9. Overcome fear. Fear undermines vision. The greatest fear to overcome is the fear of failure. Vision skills are vital for overcoming this reluctance to take risks. Fear of failure is normal, but leaders cannot allow it to paralyze them or to absorb the energy needed to pursue the vision.

Consider the tremendous feat of Mark McGwire of the St. Louis Cardinals in 1998. Hitting 70 home runs was a vision few people could imagine. Yet America watched in anticipation as each ball left the park. Mark McGwire will be remembered as one of the great home run hitters of all time. But as good as he was, he was also among the league leaders in strikeouts.

Leaders in search of a vision must learn to deal with failure. If they can't cope with failure, they can't lead.

John Belushi, the comic whose genius was cut short by fatal drug abuse, had a catch phrase he loved to bellow at people: "Wise up!" On the night of Belushi's death, newscaster Dan Rather summed up the comedian's time on earth by reminding America of Belushi's injunction to "wise up!" and closed his epitaph with this observation: "He never did."[8]

How important are vision skills? Absolutely vital. If we don't "wise up" as pastors and leaders in this new millennium, we won't survive.

It was story time at the local elementary school, and the students had been asked to share stories with the class. Johnny, a mischievous third-grader, was waxing eloquent about a crocodile trying to catch a turtle.

"That turtle ran so fast," Johnny emphasized, "he almost ran over a *Buick* on the road in front of him!"

The teacher interrupted, "Uh, Johnny—turtles don't run."

Johnny shrugged his shoulders and replied with wide-eyed enthusiasm, "Not usually! But this one didn't have a choice!"

We don't have a choice. Kingdom business is at hand. We need visionary leadership for a new millennium.

3

COMMUNICATION SKILLS

A JUDGE WAS INTERVIEWING A WOMAN about her pending divorce. "What are the grounds for your divorce?" he asked her.

The woman replied, "About four acres and a nice little home in the middle of the property, with a stream running by."

"No," the judge said. "I mean, what is the foundation of this case?"

"The foundation is made of concrete, brick, and mortar," she responded.

"I mean," he persisted, "what are your relations like?"

"I have an aunt and uncle living here in town, and so do my husband's parents."

The judge said, "Do you have a real grudge?"

"No," she replied, "We have a two-car carport and have never really needed one."

"Please," he said, trying again. "Is there any infidelity in your marriage?"

"Yes, both my son and my daughter have CD players. We don't necessarily like the music, but the answer to your questions is yes."

"Ma'am, does your husband ever beat you up?" The judge was becoming irritated.

"Yes," she responded, "about twice a week he gets up earlier than I do."

Finally in frustration, the judge asked, "Lady, why do you want a divorce?"

"Oh, I don't want a divorce," she replied. "I've never wanted a divorce. My husband does. He said he can't communicate with me."[1]

Good communication is a vital skill for new millennium ministry. One of the authors recently took a new believer to a conference where one of the finest exegetical scholars of the day was scheduled to speak. The new Christian was informed that this event would be a life-changing experience. For two days the speaker opened the Scriptures with great insight and enthusiasm. At lunch on the second day of the conference, hours before the conclusion of this Rom. 12:2 event, the young believer, hamburger in hand, asked, "What in the world is this guy talking about?"

The speaker had been explaining what it means to be part of the *ekklesia*, meaning the "called-out-ones." But he lacked the skill needed to reach this new member of that ekklesia. He spoke about momentous changes in our value system and how we must turn to the *theo-pneustos*—Word of God—for our answers. But learned as the speaker was and as exegetically sound as his presentation was, he simply wasn't communicating effectively.

Was the speaker passionate about his subject? Absolutely. Was he knowledgeable? Without doubt. Was he connecting with the audience? No, at least not with everyone.

This is an age that calls for *communicators*, not just *preachers*. Paul's advice to young Timothy still stands: "Preach the Word; be prepared in season and out of season; correct, rebuke and encourage—with great patience and careful instruction" (2 Tim. 4:2). But in light of the great communication technology of the age, the apostle would encourage the Timothys of this day to "preach to communicate."

Stay True to the Bible

For a pastor, no communication can be effective unless it's biblically sound. Even if the preacher does connect with the audience, the message will have no eternal impact if it doesn't stay true to the Bible.

James Ryle, speaking at a 1998 Promise Keepers event in the old War Memorial Stadium in Little Rock, Arkansas, gave an impassioned plea for the Church to return to the Bible as the only source of absolute truth. He brought the point home by reading from the United States Government Peace Corps manual that was given to volunteers in the Amazon Jungle. The manual told volunteers what to do in case they encountered an anaconda, the largest snake in the world. A relative of the boa constrictor, this mammoth serpent grows to 35 feet in length and weighs between 300 and 400 pounds. It's a telephone pole with a bad attitude! Here's the list of instructions for dealing with an anaconda:

1. Do not run. The snake is faster than you.
2. Lie flat on the ground. Put your arms tight against your sides, your legs tight against one another. Tuck your chin in.
3. The snake will come and begin to nudge and climb over your body. Don't panic.
4. After the snake has examined you, it will begin to swallow you from the feet end—always from the feet end. Permit the snake to swallow your feet and ankles. Don't panic. The snake will then begin to suck your legs into its body.
5. You must lie perfectly still. All of this will take a long time.
6. When the snake has reached your knees, slowly, and with as little movement as possible, reach down, take your knife, and very gently slide it into the side of the snake's mouth—between the edge of its mouth and your leg. Then, suddenly rip upwards, slicing the snake's head.
7. Be sure you have your knife.
8. Be sure your knife is sharp.[2]

The Bible is described as being "sharper than any double-edged sword" (Heb. 4:12). Nearly two centuries ago C. H. Spurgeon was quoted as saying, "A Bible that is falling apart usually belongs to a person who is not!" That being true, we need to keep our knives sharp to give people access to the Word of God by our communication.

Simple Communication Theory

Communication was never intended to be difficult. But differences in generation, gender, and worldview have made it a challenge to communicate effectively. The following shows how to simplify the communication process.

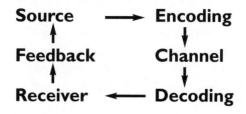

1. *All communication begins with a source.* The pastor as preacher is a source of communication. The pastor prays, studies, and reads, doing everything possible to be true to the Scriptures. As he or she thinks about (encodes) the message, the goal is to make it relevant to the people. This "encoded" truth is then presented to the audience. The presentation may use only spoken words, or it may be enhanced by technologies such as a PowerPoint presentation or some other audiovisual tool. Either way, the preacher provides a communication channel to the audience. The people who listen will then seek to understand (decode) the message. They will have a "filter" of personal perspectives, problems, and pressures through which they will listen. Their hearts and minds (the "receivers") then tackle the application of the message.

2. *Real change will never happen in a person's life until he or she not simply hears the Word, but also receives the*

message. That's why the apostle James wrote, "Do not merely listen to the word, and so deceive yourselves. Do what it says. Anyone who listens to the word but does not do what it says is like a man who looks at his face in a mirror and, after looking at himself, goes away and immediately forgets what he looks like" (James 1:22-24).

3. *The final step in the communication process is feedback.* The "communication loop" isn't complete until the listener responds. Feedback can be verbal, such as an "Amen!" "Come on, Pastor!" "Preach it!" Or it may be nonverbal. Body language, for example, is a very precise source of feedback.

The following chart offers some insights into this nonverbal feedback.

What to look for in the audience	What it usually means	
	Listener agrees, likes	*Listener disagrees, is bored*
Posture	Sitting forward, leaning in, arms relaxed	Leaning away, arms crossed over chest
Hands	Relaxed, open, taking notes	Clasped, holding on, clenched fist, fingers drumming
Seating	Closer	Hiding, farther away
Eyes	Looking at speaker	Rolling, looking away, reading bulletin
Face	Smiling, nodding, looking interested	Frowning, looking angry, looking away or uncertain

Problems in Communication

Communication is never simple, but it's not an impossible task. Good communication does demand constant evaluation, such as whether or not a connection has been made between the source and the receiver. The following are six common problems that affect a pastor's ability to communicate.

Words. Words get in the way. For example, each generation has its own vocabulary. These are the terms and lingo that are characteristic of that generation. Also, certain disciplines have their own language. Law has its vocabulary. Medicine has its own jargon. Words from a specialized vocabulary rarely retain the same meaning when they cross disciplines.

Religion also has specific terminology that has been accepted and taught for centuries. "Eschatology," for instance, comes from the Greek word *eschatos*, meaning "last things." So eschatology is the study of the last days. Another classical term, "harmartiology," is the study of sin. It's a word that comes from the root word *harmartia,* which means "missing the mark." Sin, then, causes us to *miss the mark* and fall short of God's glory and standards (Rom. 3:23). Both words are highly significant to Christian doctrine, but neither is commonly used in modern speech. The older saints in our churches may have some knowledge of these terms and may expect their inclusion in the Sunday sermon. But to generations X and Y, they are words from some foreign language, and their use may actually inhibit learning.

Older Bible translations may have a similar effect. Very few people today use such "King James" words as "verily," "hitherto," "thee," "thou," or "hast." Someone who reads "David's countenance fell" might wonder what he dropped!

Attention Span. A second frustration for a communicator is the fact that very few audience members are actually listening. The average adult attention span is between 9 and 11 minutes. But the average sermon is 30 minutes long, with three points and a good joke or story between each point. As we say elsewhere, the time frame of the average television program has influenced the "listener fence" in our church services.

Though the "average sermon time" is basically the length of a television sitcom, the communicator must understand that the audience may "change channels" during the presentation. In fact, in broadcasting it's generally understood that the audience changes every 15 minutes.

Fortunately, your audience probably won't walk out after 15 minutes—at least not physically. But some will be mentally putting on their coats if the preaching isn't really communicating.

Different "Grids." A third dilemma in communication involves the personal *grid* of the receiver. People come from different backgrounds—social, ethnic, racial, and educational. The audience's background directly affects its listening and learning. For example, an audience composed mostly of persons having postgraduate degrees would be more apt to appreciate a presentation that includes statistics, quotes from well-known authors, and theological or philosophical issues. On the other hand, an audience made up mostly of persons having little or no higher education would be more apt to learn from a simple, well-told story with application. Of course, every communicator should make practical applications of truth by using relevant illustrations.

Baggage. Another factor affecting listener response may be called "spiritual Samsonite." Every member of the audience carries a certain amount of personal baggage. Whether it's the fresh memory of a heated discussion before the service, the deeply buried memory of childhood abuse, or something in between, every audience member carries mental or emotional luggage that will affect *what* he or she hears and *how* he or she hears it.

Many congregations have members who are socially dysfunctional and are either trying to work through problem areas or are actively in denial.

Added baggage may include a chronic physical problem. A listener with a bad back, for instance, will be less likely to learn from the communicator while he or she is sitting on a hard pew or chair and the sermon or lesson presentation has passed "high noon."

Information overload. It's Sunday morning. People wake up listening to the radio, probably tuned to an "all bad news" station. They may continue by watching "Headline News" on television as they eat breakfast and dress for church. They may even scan the newspaper before leaving the house, or they may check the news on the Internet.

Once in the car, they flip on the radio for the drive to church. They may listen to a music station—anything from the top 40 to the "oldies"—or a news and commentary program. Thinking about the music, lyrics, or news, they arrive at church and are handed a bulletin with a half-dozen inserts. They now "prepare" for the service—which will include more information—by ingesting the latest church news. That involves sorting through the bulletin information and applying the list of coming events to their calendars for the coming week. *Too much data!* By the time the pastor gets up to speak, there is very little if any RAM[3] left on the listener's mental computer.

Skepticism. Our audiences are more suspicious than they have ever been and, in most instances, rightly so. Many of your listeners have been disillusioned. Some have been disappointed by their politicians. Some have been let down by respected religious leaders. Some of their favorite entertainers have even disappointed them. As a result, they're on the lookout for character and integrity flaws in those who communicate with them. Until they develop trust in those communicators, listeners will decode their message through a filter of suspicion.

Doing the Legwork

Most of the people in our churches have no idea of what it takes to put a sermon together. Pastors frequently hear the following misguided question and comments:

- "Must be great to have to work only one day a week!"

- "Have you ever wondered if you're overpaid for the hours you put in?"
- "What do you do the rest of the week?"

In reality, the preaching-communicating task is a difficult one. Every Monday morning the preacher knows that he or she will be required to come up with informative, biblical, personal, and applicable material that will suit the varied tastes of the audience—*just like last week!* The pressure can be overwhelming. That's why doing the legwork for next Sunday's presentation is vital. The speaker must be prepared in order to communicate effectively. Here are some basic steps in sermon preparation:

1. Prayer. A conversation with the Great Communicator should be at the beginning of every communication task. Prayer will do three things for sermon preparation.

First, it will open the preacher's eyes to new scriptural insights. Any pastor can tell you about a time when he or she prayerfully opened the Bible and read a familiar passage but suddenly sensed God speaking directly to his or her heart. Our Lord wants to talk to us, but our busy lives prevent us from listening. Job was reminded of that when Elihu said, "Hear my words, you wise men; listen to me, you men of learning. For the ear tests words as the tongue tastes food. Let us discern for ourselves what is right; let us learn together what is good" (Job 34:2-4).

Second, prayer will make us spiritually sensitive to the needs of people. God has placed upon every pastor the call to be a *shepherd*. Shepherds are aware of the needs of their sheep and respond appropriately. As a pastor prays for his or her people and for their specific needs, his or her heart becomes sensitive to the Lord's prompting and of appropriate Bible passages that offer help and encouragement.

Third, prayer will be personally life changing. God does not sit by some celestial cell phone waiting for us to call with suggestions for His next big decision. That's not what prayer is all about. Instead, God wants to warm our hearts and create within us a yearning to know Him better. Investing time in prayer is investing time in life change. The psalmist said it like this: "As the deer pants for streams of water, so my soul pants for you, O God" (Ps. 42:1).

2. Study. The next important step in sermon preparation is a commitment to spend time in focused study. Some of the great preaching pastors have noted the significant change in the pastoral role—including the floor plan of the pastor's church. In the evolutionary process of ministry, the "pastor's study" has become the "office." Though that's not a new observation, it's significant. The "one-size-fits-all" demands of modern ministry have seen a shift away from the "spiritual" to the "temporal." In many churches, the pastor is seen as the pastor-administrator instead of the pastor-preacher. More and more time is spent "pushing paper" to meet the demands of administration than perusing the Word of God to meet the spiritual needs of the people.

The result: spiritual famine. In some cases, listeners bring their spiral-bound notebooks to the service and wait with open Bibles for some truth that will take them through the week. Sadly, they often close both the notebook and the Bible after a few minutes of trite sermonizing that often doesn't focus on God's Word.

New millennium ministry will face obsolescence unless there is a drastic return to the study and presentation of the Word of God. "Do your best to present yourself to God as one approved, a workman who does not need to be ashamed and who correctly handles the word of truth" (2 Tim. 2:15).

"Lite" sermons won't satisfy the spiritual cravings of this generation. They want the meat of God's Word. The strongest preaching centers in modern Christianity have a strong exegetical preaching emphasis.

The effective communicator's study habits will include the following:

      Reading (both online and "hard copy")
        Bible

> Christian magazines and professional journals
> Newspapers and news magazines

Clipping and filing

> Clipping or scanning relevant passages or articles and storing them in carefully marked file folders or computer files

Watching and listening

> Audiotapes and videotapes
> Christian Internet sites

Outlining and scripting

> Attention-getting introduction
> Relevant and simple main points
> Humor and stories that apply main points
> Inspiring close

Practicing (in front of a mirror if possible)

> Deliver sermon from memory or manuscript
> Think of gestures and movement
> Concentrate on eye contact
> Practice inflection (to avoid monotone delivery)
> Check approximate times

3. Personal Preparation. Prayer time and study time are only part of the communication process. A whole range of experience outside the pastor's study directly influences effective communication.

Journal your personal experiences. Paul wrote in 2 Cor. 1:3-4, "Praise be to the God and Father of our Lord Jesus Christ, the Father of compassion and the God of all comfort, who comforts us in all our troubles, so that we can comfort those in any trouble with the comfort we ourselves have received from God." Paul was advising ministers to encourage others by drawing from the well of their own experiences. The experience of the communicator makes him or her more credible to the audience. For instance, after losing a loved one to death (both authors' fathers are deceased), it's impossible to participate in a funeral without feeling the pain of the mourners.

Observe the experiences of others. A careful observance of everyday life builds relevance into lesson and sermon presentation. It provides the "personal" dimension. Watch parents interacting with their children. It will yield useful observations for preaching. Draw illustrations from the experiences of normal life, such as stress, freeway gridlock, financial worries, health problems, or crises in the home.

Observe the faces of people as you walk through the mall, stand at the checkout counter, or sit in the airport. See how the world's values versus the Lord's values are influencing them. Reflect on the importance of that struggle. "Do not love the world or anything in the world. If anyone loves the world, the love of the Father is not in him. For everything in the world—the cravings of sinful man, the lust of his eyes and the boasting of what he has and does—comes not from the Father but from the world" (1 John 2:15-16). Personal observations from the "marketplace" will make your message informative, interesting, and relevant.

Study available data. Surveys are one powerful tool in these times of paradigm shifting. Gallup polls, for instance, offer great insights into people and their priorities in the secular world. Gallup polls on Christian values and the influence of the Church also provide the speaker with pertinent facts that add relevance to the message. Even *Reader's Digest, Family Circle, Time,* and *U.S. News & World Report* offer significant statistical glimpses into our world. Of course, be aware of the error factor in polls. Every published collection of data has its flaws.

Plan your reading. If a speaking schedule is planned well enough in advance, the speaker's reading of books, magazines, newsletters, and journals can add material to the presentation. *The Reader's Guide to Periodical Literature* is a great tool in providing an index of articles to more than 150 of the most popular magazines and journals. Encyclopedias and statistical sources (print, compact disk, or the Internet) are also good places to gather information. And religious literature is filled with great resources that support historical context, demographics, and political influences.

Also, the Internet can open doors to a whole new world of humor, statistics, stories, biographies, and other information. It even allows networking with other communicators. Many libraries now provide directions for traveling along this "information superhighway." In fact, if you're not familiar with the Internet, the library is a good place to start.

One important issue in using outside sources concerns the citing of those sources. It's not difficult to insert the source of your research into your sermon without upsetting the flow. This will demonstrate not only the depth of your research but also the breadth of your credibility.

Use a variety of sources in sermon preparation. But don't clutter the message by citing too much reference materials. The simplest way to present research in a lesson or sermon is like this:

"Billy Graham in his book _____ wrote, "_____."

"If you've read the cover article of *Time* magazine this month, you've read that _____."

"One Bible scholar, [name], wrote the following about this passage: _____."

The bottom line is this: Effective communication requires current and relevant auxiliary information. A good communicator must have an arsenal of resources at his or her disposal. And it doesn't hurt to ask other, more experienced communicators for their help or to check with the new kids on the block—recent graduates from seminary and Bible school who are adept in the latest research technologies.

Improving Communication Skills

You're very familiar with the phrase "And in conclusion." And you probably know what it means: *absolutely nothing.* For the most part, the "conclusion" is usually an introduction for another point or two. But let's try to summarize some of the communication skill material with our own "Ten Commandments of Communications":

1. *Develop a worldview.* Exegete the Word with world events in mind. An effective communicator not only has a grasp of God's *Word* but also knows what's happening in God's *world.* World events are windows through which the light of the enduring Word of God may be shown. When the speaker uses an observation about a current event as the introduction to a Bible study, the listener can better apply the historical truth of the Bible to his or her life.

2. *Make it brief.* Gone are the days of the 60-minute message. And gone are the days of the six-year series on the Gospel of Matthew! Modern communicators must understand that this is the "instant-on" age and that long, drawn-out presentations are subject to an "instant-off." When the communicator learns to say it with fewer words, in fewer minutes, over a shorter time-span, he or she has a greater chance of connecting with the audience.

3. *Stay focused.* Use a communication *rifle* rather than a communication *shotgun.* What single idea should the audience carry with them out the church door? Often communicators attempt to feed a seven-course sermon to a people who are hungry for an appetizer. Spiritual indigestion will result. Don't try to present too much material in one message or lesson. Focus on a primary truth. Avoid rambling over many truths. Don't be afraid to ask for feedback. It may help to have someone critique the sermons for clarity of focus.

4. *Make it practical.* Simplicity is a mark of good scholarship. Use words and phrases that the audience will understand and relate to. Avoid religious jargon. For instance, when communicating the need for sexual purity from the pointed passage of 1 Thess. 4:3, "Be sanctified," be sensitive to the fact that many listeners have no idea what *sanctification* means.

That doesn't mean that common doctrinal terms must

be eliminated. But if they *are* used, they must be briefly explained. The concept of sanctification might be introduced to an audience like this: "In 1 Thess. 4:3, the apostle Paul is telling us to turn away from the old way of life—which is characterized by lust and sexual immorality—and move toward God's standard of moral purity."

5. *Use an opening "grabber."* Book editors often say, "If a writer doesn't catch my attention in the first 20 pages, forget it!" What's true for written communication is equally true for verbal communication. Start the message with a story, a fact, or joke. It will serve as "bait" to lure the audience into the subject. A message on worry, for instance, might begin like this: "Some of you came to church today totally stressed out. In fact, here's a little quiz I'd like you to take to determine your personal need for today's message. Fill in the blanks out loud. 'I'm at the end of my _____.' 'I'm ready to throw in the _____.' 'I'm at my wit's _____.'" (Wait for the audience to answer each point.)

"Your answers tell me that you know something about living with anxiety. This message is for you! The Bible has much to say about worry. In fact, Paul said in Phil. 4:6, 'Be anxious for nothing' [NKJV]."

The audience will know the fill-in-the-blank answers immediately and will be instantly drawn into the subject of the message.

6. *Use the active voice.* Many communicators fail to connect with their audience because they deliver their sermons in the *passive voice*. Here's an example: "It has been said that people who read their Bibles have less stress in their lives." This *passive* communication alerts people to a need, but it doesn't motivate change. In the *active* voice, the same truth is shared this way: "Read your Bible—you'll have less stress." People need *direction* as well as *instruction*.

7. *Edit everything.* The first draft of a presentation is usually too long, too wide, and too high—which translates to *boring!* Good communication requires a fine tuning pro-

cess. What stories could be eliminated? Which points are irrelevant? Hone the message for clarity.

8. *Be honest.* Our world is filled with suspicion. We're skeptical of those who try to improve our social or spiritual standing with bold promises. Even some preachers "stretch the truth" (speaking "evang-elastically"). People have been burned so often that they find it hard to trust anyone. The audience is not fooled by a speaker who attempts to communicate something he or she doesn't understand. If you don't know something, it's better to admit it. Both the audience *and* the communicator will be put at ease, and trust will be won.

9. *Accept input.* Accepting information from others is critical for maintaining good communication skills. Never push away people who have information that will enhance a presentation. Use current affair magazines to stay abreast of trends. Consider allowing others to help with research.

10. *Ask questions.* Questions come in a variety of forms. First are *open* questions, in which the communicator challenges the audience with points for evaluation:

"What areas in your life are you unhappy with?"

"What do you think God is trying to teach you through the circumstances you're facing right now?"

Questions of this type challenge the listener to evaluate his or her perspectives, values, and life plans. Remember that your audience needs ample time to think through open questions.

Then we have *closed* questions. These tend to be narrowly focused. Some allow a simple "yes" or "no" answer, while others ask for short, direct answers:

"Are you happy with your life right now?"

"Isn't it time to make some changes?"

Leading questions are preferred by most skilled communicators. After a biblical presentation, the communicator will guide listeners through a process of self-evaluation and personal commitment by asking questions that lead toward a realization or decision.

"Are there areas in your life that God would not be pleased with right now?"

"Is God asking you to clean house and to receive a clean slate for the coming week?"

"Are you ready to deal with those issues right now?"

Leading questions are designed to allow the Spirit of God open access into the hearts of the listener. Never should we claim to have the kind of power and authority the Holy Spirit possesses. But through gentle prodding, a person's heart can be prepared for what the Spirit of God wants to do in his or her life.

Often our people carry their guilt because we've failed to teach them to keep "short accounts" with God. People need an opportunity to respond to the challenge God issues in their lives. For example, if we preach to the men in the church about the need to be godly husbands, a gap will likely form between their present behavior and their desired lifestyle. That's called a *guilt gap*. (See below.)

If we preach another sermon to these same men about the call of God to be godly examples to their children but do nothing to close the gap from the previous week, the guilt gap only widens.

It could have been closed by simply asking the listeners to keep short accounts with God by asking a series of open, closed, and/or leading questions and then guiding them through the process of confession and repentance.

The Age of Sight and Sound

As leaders entrusted with one of the most important responsibilities on this earth—sharing the gospel of Jesus Christ—we must constantly be on a *learning curve* to become more adept in our communication skills. We're trying to communicate with people who have been "trained" by Hollywood and Madison Avenue to be "seers" as well as "hearers." Consequently, our communication is enhanced when we use both sight *and* sound.

Additionally, the majority of North American homes have at least one personal computer. They also have ready access to compact disc players, videocassette recorders, and digital video disc (DVD) movies. Modern communicators must be conscious of the fact that audiences are media savvy. And that consciousness will influence the way a sermon or lesson is presented—including the use of high-tech hardware.

New millennium communicators will not fall behind technologically. They will put away the filmstrip projector and begin to use the video projector.

They will incorporate short video clips (carefully selected) into their presentations.

They will use PowerPoint and overhead transparencies to communicate the age-old message in fresh, new ways. Jesus, the greatest teacher, used both sight and sound to communicate sacred truth. And effective communicators have followed His example with great success.

Escalating technology and de-escalating costs have made audiovisual presentations affordable to congregations of almost any size. Granted, not every church can afford a video projector. But most churches can swing the cost of a videocassette recorder and a large-screen television monitor. Be creative. For instance, a member of the congregation could be asked to download Christian programming from a satellite network. Video clips could then be incorporated into a Sunday morning or weekday gospel presentation.

Enthusiasm!

Some pulpiteers are about as enthusiastic as a cheerleader at a morticians' college. Paul, another great communicator, advised, "Whatsoever ye do, do it *heartily,* as to the Lord, and not unto men" (Col. 3:23, KJV, emphasis added). Enthusiasm is key to effective communication. For example, contemporary evangelist T. D. Jakes can bring a crowd to a near frenzy by his enthusiastic presentation of scripture.

Neil Anderson told his students at Talbot School of Theology, Biola University, "If you're going to do anything for God, do it with some enthusiasm!" Do we really believe the message we're trying to communicate? Do we have a concern about the eternal destiny of the people we address? If so, let's get excited about the material!

Any Sunday sermon may be the final opportunity for someone to hear the Good News. How important it would be for that last opportunity to be crowned with holy enthusiasm—especially since the word "enthusiasm" comes from the two Greek words: *en* and *theos*, meaning "in God." When we're "in God" and on fire with the message He has placed upon our hearts, we'll be enthusiastic! A burning heart can't help but cast a few sparks.

I don't want to be like the preacher who went to sleep and dreamed he was preaching and woke up—and he was!

4

LEADERSHIP SKILLS

AN ENTOMOLOGIST AT A MIDWESTERN UNIVERSITY
conducted a study on the processionary caterpillar. This insect's most interesting features are its method of traveling and its leadership style. Processionary caterpillars travel as a connected unit. Each one has the ability to connect to the one in front of it. Once connected, they move in one long line, following the leader.

The scientist experimented to discover what would happen if there was no leader at the front of the line to give directions. He took an already connected family of processionary caterpillars and hooked the leader to the end of the last caterpillar in the line, forming a circle. Then he placed the caterpillars around the rim of a pot that matched the exact circumference of the connected group.

In the center of the pot were fresh mulberry leaves and plenty of water, the insect's normal dietary fare. How long would the bugs travel around the pot? There was plenty of food and water just inches away, but without a leader, they were content on going in the same direction.

The professor watched for hours, waiting for one caterpillar to break ranks. But none did! Instead, the group marched on in an undulating line until they all fell into the pot, unconscious from lack of nourishment.

Did you know that there are "processionary churches?" People march into church Sunday after Sunday, link hands during the fellowship time, and then fall into unconsciousness during the sermon! They have no ambition to break rank and reach into their community.

Why does that ecclesiastical species exist? Because there are "processionary leaders," pastors and laypersons who would rather stay in rank than create new direction.

Motivational speaker Steven Covey speaks of "producers" as those who are busy swinging a machete as they blaze their way through the jungle. He identifies "managers" as the ones who make sure the producers' machete is sharp. He presents the "leader," on the other hand, as the one who climbs the highest tree, looks around, and then yells, "We're in the wrong jungle."[1]

It's true—good management is necessary. Paul wrote in 1 Cor. 14:40, "Everything should be done in a fitting and orderly way." But new millennium ministry calls for people who will commit themselves to being more than "managers." If the local church is to advance in these days, it must be influenced by strong "leaders."

Consider these differences between a *manager* and a *leader*:

Old Manager	New Leader
1. Acts as the boss	1. Builds a team
2. Expects a chain of command	2. Works together
3. Makes all decisions	3. Fosters involvement
4. Hoards information	4. Shares information
5. Is a specialist	5. Is a generalist
6. Demands long hours	6. Expects results
7. Maintains	7. Builds
8. Focuses on today	8. Looks to tomorrow
9. Administers	9. Innovates
10. Follows orders	10. Takes charge
11. Lives in the past	11. Learns and grows
12. Focuses on numbers	12. Focuses on people

Seven Principles of Leadership

Leadership could be defined as attracting people to a cause greater than themselves and motivating them to reach their potential in support of that cause. "Attracting people" speaks to the issue of a leader's ability to draw people along. "Attracting people to a cause" indicates the leader's knowledge of where they are going, communicating a sense of direction to those following. "Attracting people to a cause greater than they are" implies that the leader has a sense of urgency concerning completion of the mission.

Modern ministers must understand not only the meaning of leadership but also leadership methods. What are the dynamics of effective leadership?

They may be seen in the following seven directives:

1. Give people freedom to create. The people you lead must have the freedom to try new things, to be innovative in their ministry roles. As a leader, you must release them to explore those innovations. "My way or the highway" is not in the vocabulary of the effective leader.

"But what if they fail?" you may ask. That goes with the freedom. Your followers need to understand that failure is a possibility. But they also need to understand that they will not be rejected if they encounter failure.

2. Give people authority, not just responsibility. Effective leaders are not micromanagers. They don't need all the details. They know how to give their associates the authority to make decisions in their area of responsibility. Giving that authority validates their worth as well as the leader's trust in them.

3. Show appreciation. Verbalize your gratitude for a job well done. All of us are motivated by the gratefulness of others. Thank-you notes and E-mail messages are great sources of encouragement. Use them generously. One large church gives quarterly awards to staff and leadership during the services or leadership functions. They obviously have some fun with these awards as demonstrated by their titles: The "Beef Jerky" award goes to the person who bites off the toughest of jobs; The "Goliath Killer" award goes to the one who has been victorious in completing a major undertaking; The "Wizard of Oz" award goes to the leader who always works behind the scenes to get the job done; and the "Barney" award is always presented to the person who has gone above and beyond the call of encouragement. Can you imagine the appreciation these leaders feel?

4. Recognize success. Public recognition is a great impetus for quality ministry. It not only affirms the effort of the worker but also helps ministry bystanders decide to volunteer their time and talents as well. The bottom line: People work harder when they know they're being both watched and appreciated. For example, Pastor Jim Williams gives a Five-Star Ministry Award each month to laypersons at Lake View Park Church of the Nazarene in Oklahoma City. As a result of this type of encouragement, Jim's church family responds in greater numbers to serve the Lord.

5. Involve people in the journey. The old model of leadership was top-down. Mandates are shoved downward like paper pills. The new model of leadership is more participation oriented. It allows people to contribute to the ministry process in program planning and implementation. When workers feel they are truly involved, they "buy into" the project or ministry and are more apt to volunteer their creativity.

6. Challenge people. Encourage them to "stretch." Help them to understand the old philosophy that some pain accompanies the gain. But you must also let them know that they are making an eternal difference. The rigor has its rewards.

7. Show compassion. Rom. 12:15 says, "Rejoice with those who rejoice, and weep with those who weep" (NKJV). Stay connected. Pray for the needs of your workers. Let them know you really care about them, and let them know you care about their families as well. Compassion is one of the more important leadership skills.

Characteristics of Great Leaders

You've heard people described as "born leaders." It refers to those who have obvious leadership qualities, who characteristically takes the lead in helping others find a solution to a certain problem or project. Is there some genetic disposition to leadership? That's for the scientist to determine. In a more practical sense, certain characteristics are common to great leaders.

1. A great leader prays. 2 Chron. 20 contains an interesting story about a leader's prayer life. Jehoshaphat was King of Israel at a time when three enemy nations were on the verge of attacking them. King "J" cried out to God and was told to "stand firm" and see a miracle!

2. A great leader has integrity. A leader must always speak the truth and have the courage to correct his or her mistakes. "I'm sorry" shouldn't be pulled from their mouth like an impacted tooth! It should be a natural expression.

Values must also be guarded. Leaders must be people of principle. Leaders of integrity understand that when they're confronted with compromise, there is always an obvious moral choice. And leaders of integrity are willing to make that choice.

3. A great leader is a learner. The pastoral profession contains two important components. The first is technical expertise, or the ability to do the job. It is important to be proficient in counseling, care-giving, teaching, preaching, recruiting, or motivating. The pastor should make every effort to grow in technical skill. The leader must never stop growing! Leaders must continually research and experiment with more effective methods to advance the kingdom of God.

But there's another important need. New millennium leaders must have an inner commitment to pass the torch along—they learn in order to teach others. They are concerned with passing the torch of leadership to the next generation.

4. A great leader has a sense of direction. Leaders know how to clarify their vision. The apostle Paul had the unique ability to focus his energies on what really mattered. First and foremost, he focused on Christ. "Follow my example, as I follow the example of Christ," he wrote in 1 Cor. 11:1.

Second, he had a spiritual focus that was undeterred by the events of time. "Not that I have already obtained all this, or have already been made perfect, but I press on to take hold of that for which Christ Jesus took hold of me. Brothers, I do not consider myself yet to have taken hold of it. But one thing I do: Forgetting what is behind and straining toward what is ahead, I press on toward the goal to win the prize for which God has called me heavenward in Christ Jesus" (Phil. 3:12-14).

Third, the apostle had a clear sense of ministry purpose. "Christ did not send me to baptize, but to preach the gospel—not with words of human wisdom, lest the cross of Christ be emptied of its power" (1 Cor. 1:17).

5. A great leader is committed. A double dose of determination is needed in order to succeed in new millennium ministry. Remember when the Israelites went to battle under the leadership of Gideon, as described in the seventh chapter of Judges? Despite his fears, he demonstrated a contagious commitment.

Gideon's plan was unorthodox. He divided his troops into three groups and gave every man a trumpet, a lamp, and an earthen pitcher.

No, he wasn't forming a praise band!

The plan was to attack the enemy at night, with each of the three units approaching the enemy camp from different directions. The pitchers were used to cover the lamps so as not to alert the enemy.

On Gideon's signal, the soldiers were to uncover their lights, blow their trumpets, and yell at the top of their lungs, "A sword for the LORD and for Gideon!" (Judg. 7:20).

The Midianites were suddenly alert! Fearing they were surrounded by a vastly army, they stumbled half asleep from their homes, falling over each other like elephants on ice skates. In the confusion, they turned on each other, actually killing one another. Of course, God had a heavy hand in the encounter, but He used a committed leader to carry out the plan.

Gideon's example is important for three reasons: first, he connected with the people. He met them face to face and personally conveyed his commitment to God's plan. Next, he never gave up, even when the situation appeared humanly impossible. He was creative in his tactics, but ultimately his confidence was in the power of God.

Third, he accepted the risks that went with his calling. Leaders in the new millennium will discover that there are a few thorns in the crowns of their achievement. Accepting the call to any ministry assignment is risky. Preaching and teaching to hungry hearts is a risk. Counseling sad and brokenhearted people is a risk. Leading people is a risk. But the benefits far outweigh the fears.

6. A great leader has a courageous faith. Probably no other biblical character is more associated with unwavering faith in God than Abraham. The Bible records an indelible epitaph for this great man—"Abraham believed God, and it was credited to him as righteousness" (Rom. 4:3). Even when all the earthly facts were in, the leader Abraham chose faith.

But Abraham's faith isn't a "stand-alone" faith. It can be developed in the life of any new millennium leader.

Developing an "Abraham Faith"

- Develop a sensitive spirit to God's leading.
- Start with the faith you presently have.
- Prayerfully claim individual promises from God's Word.
- Visualize miraculous answers to your prayers.
- Begin the "thanksgiving" even before the "realizing."
- Maintain your enthusiasm for God's power and supply.

Seven Leadership Skills

Leadership involves practice as well as theory. In fact, leadership theory without leadership practice is an exercise in futility. New millennium leaders must develop at least seven basic leadership skills:

1. Communicate constantly. A "field of dreams" style of leadership ("Build it, and they will come") is faulty—and often fatal. Effective leaders are communicators. They regularly involve people in their projects through oral and written communication.

The best-laid plans of ministry leaders are mere pipe dreams unless their followers are aware of them. Effective leaders learn how to help their associates "buy into" the master plan. But the "buy" won't take place unless there is a clear presentation of the plan.

And that presentation will have to be reinforced. Have you ever wondered why that commercial for breath mints is repeated several times during the same TV program? Advertisers understand the power of repetition. They understand that viewers often "tune out." By repeating the ads, they stand a better chance of communicating their message.

The same principle is important in ministry communications. After the primary message is communicated, to paraphrase the well-known real estate axiom, then "the most important thing is *repetition! repetition! repetition!*"

And don't forget the "late breaking news." Effective leaders understand the importance of updating their associates on changes to the master plan.

2. Preach passionately. Pastors are ambassadors of the King. And the King spoke with authority. "When Jesus had finished saying these things, the crowds were amazed at his teaching, because he taught as one who had authority, and not as their teachers of the law" (Matt. 7:28-29).

With so many confusing ideologies in this world, the message of the Kingdom should be clear. And it must also be sincere. There have been too many instances in which the character lines of the message and the messenger have been blurred.

A "Thus saith the Lord" mandate leaves no room for wishy-washy words. That "30-minute window of opportunity" allowed most modern communicators has eternal consequences. A passion to preach the Word of God is both visible and audible. If your message doesn't stir you, more than likely you'll need to have the ushers pass out anti-drowsiness tablets to stir anyone else in the sanctuary!

Paul's advice to Timothy still stands: "Preach the Word; be prepared in season and out of season; correct, rebuke and encourage—with great patience and careful instruction" (2 Tim. 4:2).

3. Respect everyone earnestly. The people to whom you minister are unique creations of God. They have God-given characteristics. They have God-given understanding. They have God-given abilities (and inabilities). God looked over *all* His creation and declared that it was good. The job of His ambassadors, then, is to *find* the good and *affirm* that good in those who come under their area of responsibility. Granted, sometimes the search is exhausting! But it's there. The stamp of the divine image is on every child of the Father. We should be faithful "postal inspectors!"

Peter the apostle gave some very practical advice to ministry leaders, "Show proper respect to everyone: Love the brotherhood of believers, fear God, honor the king" (1 Pet. 2:17). Effective leadership doesn't parade favoritism around. We're human, of course. And humans have a tendency to gravitate to those who share their ideals and interests. But New Testament Christianity is built on common ground. "For we were all baptized by one Spirit into one body—whether Jews or Greeks, slave or free—and we were all given the one Spirit to drink" (1 Cor. 12:13-14).

4. Share information honestly. If generation X and Y are teaching us anything, it's that they won't feast on "phony baloney." They're looking for the genuine. For example, "holy tone" preaching is as outmoded as a lime-green leisure suit in these days. And new millennials are not that intrigued with the numbers on the maple veneer attendance board in the front of the sanctuary. They want to see how much of the church is in those who are attending! They want real faith, not virtual faith.

Whether we like it or not, "tabloid Christianity" is still making its impact on ministry. Those who have so spectacularly fallen off the pedestals of time are still influencing those whom we are trying to influence. Consequently, a very transparent leadership is mandatory.

Hidden agendas and buried numbers will certainly be discovered in these new millennial days. This is the *60 Minutes* era, when people demand to be "in the know." Leaders must be careful to be factual in their content and presentation.

5. Follow through carefully. Good follow-through is important in the game of golf. Membership in an exclusive country club or dressing in the latest golf fashion doesn't make a great game of golf. In fact, you can have the most expensive set of clubs on the course and still not play a decent golf game without a good swing and follow-through. We're told that what happens *after* the swing is as important as the swing itself. The follow-through is important to the direction of the ball.

Follow-through is an important leadership skill as well. You can have motivation, purpose, and plans and still accomplish very little.

The aim is important, and the launch is important. But the real success comes in the follow-through. An important leadership survival skill is the ability to follow up on the details of the project. Periodic checks on the personnel, the resources, and the progress of a project helps to insure its direction toward the goal.

6. Train repeatedly. There is little excuse in these days for dull ministry skills. Almost every day we receive notice of some area seminar or workshop. Christian television and radio schedules are dotted with programs to help us further our ministry education. Ministry books and magazines are focused on helping us minister. The library card is still free! And most denominations offer continuing education courses. The opportunity is there. Taking advantage of it is our responsibility.

Technology is changing almost daily. By the time you get your new computer unpacked, the company that manufactured it has announced a new model! Personnel working in the information technology fields express worried concern about staying ahead of their game. If they're concerned about honing temporal skills, ministry leaders should be more concerned about those skills that affect the eternal.

New millennium leaders should always be in training camp. Coach Paul said, "Do you not know that in a race all the runners run, but only one gets the prize? Run in such a way as to get the prize. Everyone who competes in the games goes into strict training. They do it to get a crown that will not last; but we do it to get a crown that will last forever" (1 Cor. 9:24-25).

7. Praise profusely. All of us are anxious for the day we will hear that word of greeting from the Savior, "Well done." But it might be nice to hear it once in awhile this side of glory. Actually, ministry leaders can be the Master's voice in expressing praise for a job well done. New millennium leaders understand the importance of giving their associates a verbal pat on the back.

This is a very impersonal age. In most cases, our lives are reduced to a series of digits—the bumps and valleys of code that allow a message to be broadcast digitally. For many, life is a nine-to-five sentence in a corkboard-and-carpet cubicle of a windowless office. And most of the residents assume that the "neighbor" in the next cubicle is still alive!

Modern employees can go through a day, week, or

month without ever hearing a "Well done." Just think how important it is to operate on a higher level than that in our ministries. In fact, encouragement is mandated in the Scriptures: "Encourage one another and build each other up" (1 Thess. 5:11).

That's the mandate. What are the methods? They are both numerous and obvious.

Handshake
Telephone call
Note
Letter
E-mail
Lunch
Coupons or tickets
Day off

Encouragement and praise just may be one of the most important factors in the success of new millennium leaders.

A feature on television's *60 Minutes* examined the day that United States President Abraham Lincoln was shot. They itemized the things found in Lincoln's pockets, which included a pocketknife and some money. But additionally, the show reported, in his wallet was a yellowed newspaper clipping that he apparently had saved for some time. It was an editorial by a British writer named Bright, who had written that though most Americans were criticizing Lincoln, he thought he would go down as one of America's greatest presidents. Evidently, Abraham Lincoln saved that clipping and read it often.

The president needs it. Your superior needs it. Your parents or children need it. Your students need it. The young person bagging your groceries needs it. Your Sunday School teacher, nursery workers, maintenance people—hey, we *all* need it!

5

CHANGE SKILLS

CHANGE AGENTS ARE USUALLY considered mavericks. They continually think "outside the box" and are willing to stretch traditional ideas. But change agents are necessary to the evolution of any organization. They redefine the old formulas. They are candid in their desire to improve and to excel. They push the envelope.

Though the builder generation has been suspect of change agents, baby boomers have usually given them their respect. French skier Jean-Claude Killy is a prime example of a change agent. Killy made the French national ski team for the first time in the early 1960s. He knew full well that he would have to work longer hours and maintain a grueling pace if he were to excel on the slopes. He lifted more weights than anyone else, ran more sprints than his teammates, and put his body to the test more often than any other athlete on the French Team.

But Killy was also a change agent in his sport. He realized that muscles and endurance were important but that training alone would never put him on top—he needed an edge. He began to challenge popular theories of the day regarding ski racing. Nothing was beyond his curiosity, and he often tested different techniques trying to discover the edge he needed. He began skiing with his legs slightly apart, totally contrary to the accepted strategy of the day. He "sat back" on his skis as he turned, always searching for a few more miles per hour. These innovations propelled him to the top of his field.

By the mid-1960s Jean-Claude Killy had won every major skiing event. He then proceeded to win three gold medals in the Winter Olympics, an achievement that has never been topped. The sport of ski racing was radically changed by his willingness to question the norm and challenge the status quo.

What's true in the sporting world is even more of a reality in the Church world. If we're to maneuver on the fresh fallen snow of this new millennium, we must be willing to evaluate our way of doing ministry and decide if constructive change is necessary. And, of course, that assessment must be filtered through the grid of relevancy and effectiveness. Change skills are necessary for survival.

Change Is Happening

Look around. Change may be the only constant in our society. Education has changed. Politics have changed. Cultural standards have changed. Since our society is continually changing, what are the forces in that society that the Church must reckon with?

Growth in Technology. Technology has come to Church. And it's about time! America has been a media-oriented culture for more than 35 years. And the overwhelming influence of the media has influenced our church services. For example, since we now minister to people with short audio and visual attention spans, cutting-edge pastors are preaching timeless truths in three 8- to 9-minute segments, with plenty of illustrative material and perhaps a PowerPoint outline projected on the screen in the front of the sanctuary.

Note: Communicators who refuse to change their presentation to appeal to short attention span-ers will soon be talking primarily to church furniture—pews, not people.

And thanks to that same media influence, second-rate technology is not acceptable. It's time to store the flannelgraph in the attic! Over half of America's homes have access to the Internet. It's the interactive age. Colorful graphics and digital sound are the norm. Vibrant ministries aren't reading letters from missionaries on the field in their missions conventions—they're providing a direct link. And more than likely, that missionary will be giving the on-site report from his or her cell phone.

Of course, budgetary restrictions will limit the scope of our use of technology. But what is affordable and what is effective should be utilized to present the ageless message of the gospel to this new age.

Demographic changes. Churches do not minister in a vacuum. They reflect their culture. And the changing demographics of the culture are mind-boggling. Here are a few examples.

Gender demographics have changed. Women aren't just part of the workforce—in many cases they're leading it! Many of them have broken through the glass ceiling and have become the CEOs of their companies. The Church, once dependent on women volunteers in its ministry, must now look to other volunteer sources or adjust its ministries and schedules to incorporate those leaders.

Ethnic demographics have changed. We're now a multi-ethnic society. In some parts of our major metropolitan areas, English is almost a foreign language. In this new millennium the Church will have to adapt to cross-cultural ministry. Many vibrant churches are already there. For example, some are planting new language-specific ministries or at least adding new services.

ESL (English as a second language) classes have become one of the most effective outreach ministries of the Church. With immigrants wanting to join the workforce, their need to understand and speak English has provided a prime opportunity for the Church to provide classes—and even use the Bible as a textbook.

First Korean Church of the Nazarene in Nashville was birthed through the teaching of English as a second language. During the time of Stan Toler's ministry, the congregation relocated to Antioch, Tennessee. Amazingly, Pastor Kee Chae Han started a second service as an outreach to the English-speaking community and renamed the church Calvary Chapel Church of the Nazarene to reflect a broader outreach!

Population demographics have changed. Driven by the breakdown of the family and the increase in crime, some are escaping the pressures of city life. Rural rebound is in full force! Ultraskilled workers are leaving the urban "rat race" for nonskilled positions in sleepy suburbia.

In other cases, an urban revival is underway. Major cities are renovating their downtown areas. Generation X is packing up and moving downtown. Businesses and entertainment have sensed the move and have provided glitzy new climes. The churches that have abandoned the city must now rethink their location, or at least consider a "downtown" extension ministry.

Age demographics have changed. The gray hairs are taking over! The rising median age has drastically changed our culture. Willard Scott will have to come out of retirement to devote more time to greeting those who have reached 100. And churches will need to adapt their ministries to meet the needs of this growing age-group. For example, where the search for a youth pastor used to be a priority, it now may be just as important to add a staff member who ministers to retirees.

And the over-60s age-group has become a great volunteer pool. Industry knows it. Healthcare knows it. Retail knows it. And Wal-Mart has known it for a long time! If their workers can give you a smile and a shopping cart, why can't the church recruit some greeters and ministry workers in the same way?

Social demographics have changed. The once-secure sources for health and welfare are fading. Many people are now looking to the Church to provide the assistance that government once provided. In fact, many government agencies and the United States president are referring to the Church. Effective leaders are recognizing the change as a tremendous opportunity. Filling in the health and welfare gaps can be a vital source for presenting the gospel—along with a grocery bag of food.

Financial insecurity. People have more money today than they have ever had, but they seem to be enjoying it less. They find themselves surfing the Internet or watching the crawler across the bottom of their TV screen to catch the latest ups or downs of the stock market. For no matter how much money is available—as Baby Boomers have become acutely aware—it may not be enough for retirement. In fact, insecurity about health care and housing costs is common.

Declining morality. The Church is sadly weak and ineffective at counteracting a senses-driven culture. Even the Disney domain profits from low-morals television and movie ventures. And the Web has replaced the corner adult bookstore as the place to satisfy the sensual.

Sadly, the Church not only is ineffective in countering this culture but also in some cases has succumbed to it. Polls reveal that moral behavior among those within the Church is often on par with that of the world.

Spiritual skepticism. Secular humanism is becoming the dominant factor in our society. Its tentacles reach into the courts, into the classrooms, and into the city or county buildings. It's not content until all vestiges of faith have been sandblasted from the architecture or banished from the front lawns of our government property.

Skeptics have not barred the doors of our churches, but they have brought such derision and scorn to the faithful that churchgoing is considered unfashionable. That's not a new idea, but it's quickly becoming a force to reckon with.

Suspicion of Leadership. From Watergate to Whitewater, modern political leaders have let us down. The suspicions resulting from their behavior has settled into our society. Everyone from the governor to the local dogcatcher is thought to have a hidden agenda.

But the letdown isn't limited to politics. High-profile scandals have touched the Church as well. In some respects, the local church still lives under the clouds brought on by the failures of numerous well-known television evangelists.

Initiating Change in the Church

Coming to grips with these changes in our society is a focal point for the Church. Though its message must not change, its ministries will have to be adjusted to the times. And often those adjustments become speed bumps on the highway of life. The following appeared recently in *Net Results* magazine:

- When trains were first invented, several "experts" agreed that if a train went at the frightful speed of fifteen miles per hour, the passengers would get nosebleeds and they would suffocate when going through tunnels.

- In 1881, the New York YMCA announced typing lessons for women. Protests were made on the grounds that the female constitution would break down under the strain.

- When the telephone was first invented, Joshua Coppersmith was arrested in Boston for trying to sell stock in a company which would build them. The "experts" said that all well-informed people know it is impossible to transmit the human voice over a wire.[1]

Obviously we survived all of those newfangled ideas. The problem of acceptance wasn't in the innovation—it was probably in the presentation. New ideas need to be presented carefully. And in the case of the Church, new ideas need to be presented both carefully and *prayerfully*.

The key to effective change is to initiate it properly. But

first, new millennium leaders must understand the varieties of change that may take place in ministry.

There are five kinds of change:

1. Tentative Change. The following diagram reflects tentative change.

Here's an example of tentative change. A pastor is called to serve a very traditional church. The members are content with the size, outreach, and ministries of the church. Therefore, the new pastor makes an effort to enhance, improve, and perpetuate traditional programming. Tentative change occurs when a leader makes only minor adjustments to maintain the status quo.

2. Turbulent Change. Turbulent change looks like this.

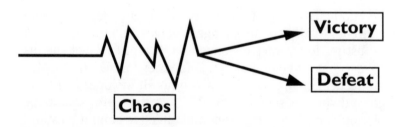

Turbulent change usually takes place when drastic modifications are introduced into a situation that appears to be going smoothly. The leadership team may not be satisfied with the direction of the ministry. So a visit to an innovative church or attendance at a church growth seminar may follow.

The leaders return to their own church and immediately begin to institute some of the innovations they have been exposed to. Instant chaos! The music is different. The sermons are altered. The choir robes are burned. The piano is moved, and the organ is put into the basement.

After the gunfire has subsided and the Sunday School bus in the parking lot has been turned right side up, the leader faces the music. The pastor is either victorious or defeated—a *hero* or a *zero*. Sadly, "chaotic change" is probably the most common change in North American churches.

3. Tactical Change. The third change can be diagrammed like this:

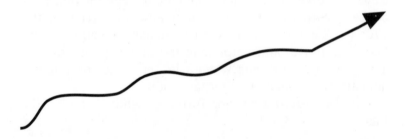

Tactical change is actually the standard in growing churches. This type of change involves fine-tuning present ministries for greater effectiveness. It also involves the discovery and launching of new ministries for added growth.

Tactical change is much smoother. It includes laying the groundwork of seeking the mind of the Lord, long-range planning, careful delegation, and effective communication.

4. Transitional Change. Transitional change may be illustrated like this:

Transitional change occurs where there's an "old" way of doing things that's clearly established and a "new" way of doing things that is preferred. The first step is to unfreeze the old thinking. Education is provided and models presented to demonstrate how the "new" way would look. The congregation either leaps, crawls, or is pushed across the chasm of change to the new way, but then "refreezes" by codifying the change as a *new* status quo.

Leaders must understand that some of the congregation will remain on the "old" side of the chasm. And their influence remains as a force for "un-change." Constantly reinforcing the benefits of the "new" will help, but not always solve, the attitude of the "chosen refrozen."

5. Transformational Change. The final, and perhaps the most desired, type of change is transformational change. It looks like this.

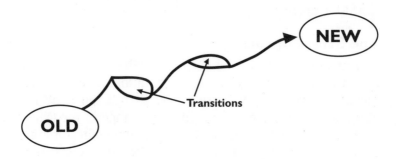

Transformational change is a combination of the "tactical" and "transitional" approaches. In this model, we have a known "old" and a preferred "new." Initial change is implemented but begins to lose momentum. Before the momentum is lost, however, a "second curve" is started. After a period of transition, the second curve recovers toward more effective ministry.

Later the momentum begins to slip again. After another period of transition, another corrective curve is initiated. The process continues as the leader guides the church through a series of transitions toward the goal of effective ministry.

This kind of change requires two things. First, it calls for motivated "second curve" thinkers among the leadership who are always looking ahead. Second, it requires mature "first curve" thinkers who have the ability to stabilize and support the current ministry while future plans are laid in place.

Change is about adapting. Just as the purpose of a tadpole is to become a frog, the purpose of the Church is to evolve into a fully functioning body through the power of the Holy Spirit. If a tadpole does not become a frog, it dies. But if the tadpole grows into a frog, it will experience major changes—without losing its real tadpole essence. The Church—the Body of Christ—has been given a mission. But it has also been given a window of opportunity to accomplish that mission. It's time to make the ministry-method changes that are needed to help the Church reach a lost world for Christ.

The Stress of Change

Anyone who has tried to improve his or her physical health by running is aware of a condition called a "stress fracture." The stress fracture is less than a full bone fracture but slightly more than a sprain. Change in the Church can create "stress fractures." For example, the timing of change is critically important. Daryl Conner offers a verbal picture of that point.

> For years, I had difficulty finding a way to convey the level of resolve that I observed winners display during change. Then one day, I watched a television news interview that said it all. At nine-thirty on a July evening in 1988, a disastrous explosion and fire occurred on an oil-drilling platform in the North Sea off the coast of Scotland. One hundred sixty-six crewmembers and two rescuers lost their lives in the worst catastrophe in the twenty-five-year history of North Sea oil exploration.

One of the sixty-three crewmembers who survived was a superintendent on the rig, Andy Mochan. His interview helped me find a way to describe the resolve that change winners manifest.

From his hospital bed he told of being awakened by the explosion and alarms. He said that he ran from his quarters to the platform edge and jumped fifteen stories from the platform to the water. Because of the water's temperature, he knew that he could survive a maximum of only twenty minutes if he were not rescued. Also, oil had surfaced and ignited. Yet Andy jumped 150 feet in the middle of the night into an ocean of burning oil and debris. When asked why he took that potentially fatal leap, he did not hesitate. He said, "It was either jump or fry." He chose possible death over certain death.[2]

There really was no choice. The price of staying on the platform—of maintaining the status quo—was too high. Something had to change.

Businesses, civic organizations, governmental agencies, and churches are often confronted with the need for radical change. But there's a risk in making that jump! Observe these potential stress points in the change process.

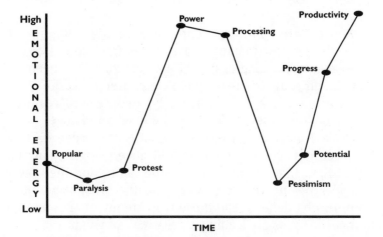

The column on the left represents the emotional energy expended by the people in your church when a radical change occurs. The bottom axis represents the time it takes for parishioners to accept the change. Notice the highs and lows, or phases of stress, experienced during change.

Phase One: Popularity. The ministry is sailing in smooth waters. It's popular. But the leadership wants to set sail for the open seas—riskier waters. So it suggests change. The congregation hasn't bought into the trip and asks the leaders, "Why upset the boat?" "Things are going along just fine." "Let's leave things the way they are." Interestingly, the church could be in a season of plateau or decline, and its leaders will continue to get those kinds of statements. The people don't see the need for change. And a stress fracture develops over changing the popular.

Phase Two: Paralysis. Just as the stress fracture immobilizes a runner, so stress changes often immobilize the congregation. The initial reaction to change is negative. Church members are shocked and confused. Suddenly the gospel ship is dead in the water. The sails have been firmly set by the leaders, but the winds of adversity are contrary.

Caution: *Before initiating any change process, a leader should remember that when any change occurs, something dies.*

Phase Three: Protest. People are openly antagonistic about the proposed changes. The stress fracture has resulted in pain. The congregational comfort zone has been invaded, and some of the people have chosen to ignore or reject the modifications. Naturally, people will respond negatively until they understand the need for change.

Phase Four: Power. Hurt turns to anger. An open fracture has occurred. People adopt the old advertising slogan "I'd rather fight than switch." The battle is on, and the power struggles begin! The "old way" and the "new way" have become a battlefield. And those who are intent on a promotion in the ranks are leading a negative campaign.

Phase Five: Processing. Some healing begins. People start bargaining with the leadership in the midst of the changes. They even begin to accept some of the changes.

Phase Six: Pessimism. Some members of the congregation consider giving up. "It sounds good, but I have my doubts." "Why are we even doing this?" Their outlook is characterized by gloom, despair, and agony.

Phase Seven: Potential. Some successes occur. People are beginning to see some possibilities. They no longer feel like victims, and they are beginning to "buy" some of the changes. There are some favorable winds back in the sails of the gospel ship!

Phase Eight: Progress. Changes have been assimilated into the church's life. Morale is elevated. The resisters are now on board.

Phase Nine: Productivity. As change is accepted, growth becomes the norm. A synergy exists between the leaders and the people. They actually begin to enjoy and support the changes—until there is another stress fracture (which is possible at any point).

Understanding Basic Change Skills

Earlier in this chapter, transformational change was offered as the best type of change. In this type of change, transitions occur between the "first curves" and the "second curves." (See below.)

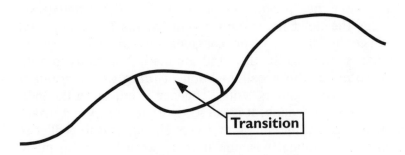

Transition

The remainder of this chapter examines the skills necessary to make smooth transitions from the first to the second curves. The following diagram illustrates the change cycle.

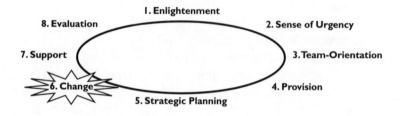

Stage 1: Enlightenment.

All changes begin with a period of enlightenment, a growth in understanding. Throughout the Bible we see how enlightenment took place before change was realized. Job's understanding of God's sovereignty helped him begin a spiritual growth even in his trials. Nehemiah was enlightened about the ruined condition of Jerusalem's walls before he launched his rebuilding crusade. Jonah certainly understood God's plan more fully when he found himself on a Mediterranean cruise in the hold of that smelly ship. Once the Jerusalem Counsel's eyes were opened to the validity of the Gentile conversions, they implemented an outreach to them.

Stage 2: Sense of Urgency

After the "period of enlightenment," the congregation sees the need for making modifications in its ministry. Once the "buy" is made, congregational members begin to discuss the possibilities. And the discussion turns to a direction. In the excellent book *Leading Congregational Change*, the authors write, "Urgency is critical in the individual organization. It creates the driving force that makes the organization willing to accept change and to challenge the conventional wisdom. It is no wonder that so many churches seem unwilling to change—they lack any sense of urgency."[3]

Stage 3: Team Orientation

The momentum leads to a master plan. The leadership is assembled for a study and implementation of the new direction. This is a crucial point in the proposed change. The leadership must act quickly while there is momentum. Based on the suggestions of the "people," a plan is offered with thanksgiving to them for their great insight. Again from *Leading Congregational Change* we read, "Transforming an established congregation, particularly one that is large or old, is a daunting undertaking. It cannot be accomplished without God and it should not be attempted as a solo enterprise of the pastor. The complexity of change and the need to mobilize the full giftedness of the body requires that a group of staff and lay leaders coalesce around the future direction of the church."[4]

Stage 4: Strategic Planning

Next comes the process of strategic planning. Howard Hendricks tells about his boyhood visits to a park to watch some older men play checkers. On one occasion, one of the men asked if Howard would like to play. He took the challenge and sat down across from the older man. At first the boy was not doing too badly. He even captured a few of the pieces from the older man. But all of a sudden the older man picked up one of his checkers and began to hop Howard's checkers. He skipped clear across the board and then exclaimed, "King me!" Once he had a king, the old fellow quickly cleared the board of Howard's checkers. That was a great lesson in long-range planning.[5] Without planning, a leader is always one turn away from being "kinged."

The Bible is full of passages on the necessity of planning. Ps. 33:11 says, "The plans of the LORD stand firm forever, the purposes of his heart through all generations."

Prov. 15:22 tells God's people, "Plans fail for lack of counsel, but with many advisors they succeed." Not forgetting
Prov. 16:3—"Commit to the LORD whatever you do, and
your plans will succeed." Planning is commended throughout the Scriptures. Robert W. Bradford and J. Peter Duncan
in their *Simplified Strategic Planning* write, "Every business
has a course and direction, just like a sailboat on the
ocean. Left alone, the boat drifts with the wind and cur-
rents. But if a captain and officers have a destination in
mind and take control of the boat, it becomes a vehicle to
get to the future, a vehicle for realizing dreams."[6]

Here's a simple model for long-range, strategic planning.

| Initial Tactics | → | Goals | → | Stretch goals | → | 5-Year Plan | ⟶ | Mission |

Stage 5: Provision

Does the change involve funding? What's the bottom-
line cost for implementing the change? Where will the
funds come from? What is the plan for involving the people in funding the suggested change?

It may include added personnel. How will the staff be
added? But as we've mentioned several times already, God
never guides where He doesn't provide. When Abraham
needed a sacrifice, God provided. When Noah needed the
rain, God provided. When our Lord wanted to feed 5,000-
plus people and all the food available wouldn't even feed
the hungry band of disciples following Him, God provided.
And as servants of the King of Kings and Lord of Lords,
rest assured: God continues to provide.

Stage 6: Evaluation

Evaluation is the final step in leading change. Three important areas should be evaluated: effectiveness, perfor-

mance, and ownership. The effectiveness of a change is evaluated first because it gets us right to the goal. Evaluating effectiveness means asking the question "Are we hitting the target?"

Next, the performance of those involved in the ministry must be evaluated. Does the team understand the changes that must be made? Are they able to execute them?

Third, a leader must analyze the ownership of change among the people. Ownership transcends buy-in. Buy-in can be reached with a series of meetings or a series of messages to increase the people's enlightenment. One meeting or one sermon explanation isn't enough to either enlighten the congregation or cause them to "buy into" the change.

The Joy of Change

It's been said that change is inevitable, except in a vending machine. If so, why is the process of change so tough for the people of God? Marilyn Ferguson has the answer: "It's not so much that we're afraid of change or so in love with the old ways, but it's that place between that we fear. It's like being in between trapezes. It's Linus when his blanket is in the dryer. There's nothing to hold on to."[7] How true! Living by faith is not easy, so change won't come easily.

But there's joy in changing and helping others to change. Glen Martin saw that joy in action following an evangelism-training course at his church. The church's leadership had one of those enlightening "Aha" moments when Glen asked the people if they knew how to share their faith. Very few did. Yes, they knew it was important, and yes, they hoped someone else was doing it. Soon Glen's team leaders were guided through the training seminar "Contagious Christianity."

One man who attended the seminar seemed particularly uncomfortable with the whole thing. "Bob" sat with arms folded in obvious defiance of the instructor. Come to find out, he sat through eight hours of training only because his wife had pressured him to attend.

The following Monday his boss asked what he had done all weekend. "Bob" reluctantly told him that he was stuck at church for most of the weekend learning how to share his faith. The boss pulled up a chair and said, "Tell me." "Bob" was stunned but went on to explain the plan of salvation. Unbelievably, he led his boss to Christ.

Guess who was the most excited man in the church the following week! He had experienced the joy of being changed and helping another to change.

For change to become long-lasting and widespread, support and reinforcement are vital. Helping people experience change goes beyond understanding, training, teamwork, and involvement. Sustaining the momentum needed for change demands continual support and constant effort. That's why we must develop the skills to initiate change if we're to pastor effectively in this new millennium.

6

ALIGNMENT SKILLS

EVERY LEADER NEEDS a little motivation at times.

The wrestling coach of a large high school in the Pacific Northwest was getting his team ready for the biggest match of the year against their closest neighbors. The state championship was at stake as they boarded the bus to go to the event.

The coach wanted to make sure they were mentally prepared and walked down the center isle of the bus to remind his team, "Men, our opposition is known for one move and one move only. It's called the double reverse. They'll bend you in one direction and then bend you in the other. And soon you won't be able to move. Your hands and arms will go numb. Your legs and feet will turn blue, and they'll have you pinned in 15 seconds. Don't get caught in the double reverse!"

The team arrived at the wrestling arena and began changing into their uniforms when the coach once again reminded them, "Men, remember, our opposition is known for one move and one move only. It's called the double reverse. They'll bend you in one direction, and then bend you in the other. And soon you won't be able to move. Your hands and arms will go numb. Your legs and feet will turn blue, and they'll have you pinned in 15 seconds. Don't get caught in the double reverse!"

The first three wrestlers were pinned by the double reverse, and the coach went ballistic. He walked up to the next wrestler and told him, "I don't care what it takes—don't get caught in the double-reverse! Run around the mat if you have to—just stay out of the double-reverse!" Thirty seconds into the match, the wrestler—you guessed it—was in the double reverse. Unbelievably, he got out of it and pinned his opponent.

The coach couldn't believe it. He ran out onto the mat and lifted his wrestler by the waist as though he had just won the gold medal in his weight class. He set the wrestler down and asked him, "How did you do it? I have to tell the rest of the team. We have a chance now to win the state championship. Tell me how you won!"

The wrestler looked the coach in the eyes and said, "Coach, it was just as you said. He bent me in one direction and then bent me in the other. And soon I couldn't move. My hands and arms were going numb. My legs and feet were turning blue, and I knew I would be pinned in 15 seconds, if I didn't do something.

"Then I saw this great big toe—right in front of my face. And I leaned forward and bit that toe just as hard as you could bite a big toe."

Then the young wrestler added, "It's amazing what you can accomplish when you bite your own big toe!"

The Power of Alignment

We don't know if you have a "big toe" on your horizon, but nonetheless there will be times when a little realignment is needed to get you back on track.

The same is true with the Church. Imagine ministering in a congregation in which the people from the staff down to the regular attendees share an understanding of the mission, vision, and goals of the church. Imagine being on a team in which every leader could clearly state the needs of your community, and every leader knows his or her role in contributing to meet those needs. The average pastor reads this and says, "Impossible!"

This chapter is all about moving toward the "impossible."

One of the leadership survival skills necessary for the new millennium is to create an internal structure that's *self-aligning*—one that frees people to utilize their personal passion and spiritual gifts to advance the kingdom of God, one that *aligns* people to use their energies both effectively and efficiently.

Alignment can be a powerful force. Our Lord spoke of it in Acts 1:8—"You will receive power when the Holy Spirit comes on you; and you will be my witnesses in Jerusalem, and in all Judea and Samaria, and to the ends of the earth."

In other words, you all have a responsibility. You will be part of the team who will reveal to a Christ-less world who I am and what I came to do on the earth.

Start in your hometown.

Move quickly to the suburbs and the greater areas around your living environment.

And never neglect the rest of the world.

Stay in alignment!

Airplane pilots talk about course variance. It's a bit unnerving to realize that many planes are slightly off course about 90 percent of the time. To prevent too much course variance, a computer is used in the ongoing process of making adjustments to keep the plane in alignment. If not enough adjustment is given, the plane will quickly get off track. And when too much adjustment is made, the same problem occurs. Alignment is a process of constant mid-course corrections.

The Dimensions of Alignment

While speaking at a men's camp in northern California, Glen was on a very tight schedule. He needed to get home to preach at his church. To help with the schedule problem and to relieve his stress, one man at the camp arranged for someone to fly him from the local landing strip to the San Francisco airport in a two-seat Cessna airplane.

The small plane landed, the luggage was loaded, and off they went. Glen thought, *What a joy! Seated in this plane, flying at low altitudes, I can see the area like I've never seen it before. And as many times as I've flown, I've never seen a landing up close and personal.*

The power and safety of alignment were seen in the small plane's approach to the San Francisco Airport. As it approached the runway, the pilot was in tune with every variable and was ready to respond to the commands of the traffic controller in the tower.

Since crosswinds affected the plane's orientation, course corrections quickly needed to be made. Airspeed was adjusted, as the flaps and throttle were gently manipulated. The pilot explained how the rate of descent and the pitch and yaw were all calibrated for a smooth landing.

All the elements were part of an interaction between the pilot, the plane, and the airport. As long as the plane aligned with the runway and was in a proper glide slope, there would be a safe touchdown. The key: constant adjustments!

In the same sense, proper *alignment* is needed in leading the church. There are two distinct dimensions of alignment: *vertical* and *horizontal*. The vertical alignment deals with the leader's personal relationship with Jesus Christ, personally seeking His will, and seeking His will for the people that He has entrusted us with. Vertical alignment includes providing strategy to meet the mission God has given them.

Horizontal alignment involves the leader's relationship with the people in the church and motivating them toward the fulfillment of the mission. This is accomplished by effective programming and laser-like focus on the target (the runway).

When the alignment is in place, a dynamic relationship naturally follows. Let's diagram alignment this way:

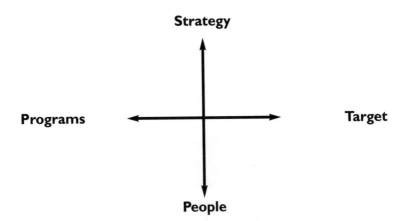

All four elements become interconnected and actually end up supporting each other. The strategy is motivating toward the target, as are the energy and drive of the people. The programs become highly supportive of the strategy and the people, and vice-versa. The alignment now looks like this:

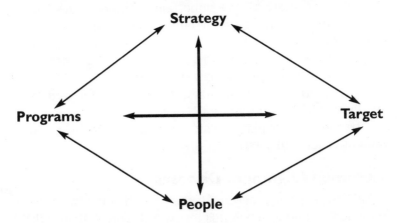

The key to maintaining this alignment is the addition of another element. They demand a "plumb line" to stay the course.

And just as the plane relies upon the computer to correct course variation, that additional element corrects "mission drift" when it's detected. Notice the addition of "mission" to the diagram:

Important Alignment Questions

For a new millennium leader to survive, he or she must examine and address three important alignment questions.

1. Will our strategy (programs) help us hit the target (our mission)?

2. Do the people support the strategy (programs), and do they understand the target (mission)?

3. Does the strategy utilize the people's gifts, and is it in alignment with our mission?

Perhaps this explains why we began with the discussion of vision skills earlier in this book.

Common Alignment Diseases

A pastor recently asked, "If the Church is the institution ordained of God to reach this lost world, why is it so sick?" Good question! Here are some of the common Church diseases that hinder proper alignment.

1. Lack of Synergism. Synergism is the process of working together. In many churches, that isn't happening. In such churches each ministry department typically has its own focus and desired results. Each works hard to achieve its own goals and to make its own difference for the Kingdom. These individual efforts are great, but they don't constitute a working-together effort. And that's a problem!

A church in Tennessee had been battling with this "turfism" for over a year. The congregation was growing and genuinely making an impact in the community surrounding Nashville. But along with the growth a lack of synergism developed. For example, their Sunday School ministry had become stagnant and unable to expand due to a competing discipleship program.

"Competing" may sound like a strange word in relation to church ministry, but it accurately describes this church's crisis. The lack of alignment played out like this: The Sunday School could not expand because discipleship programs, typically much smaller in numbers, refused to move to smaller quarters. Did they have the same goals? Absolutely. Both ministries were focused on biblical education. But there was a lack of synergism, and consequently the overall ministry of the church was out of alignment.

2. Strategic Disconnection. "Jeff" pastored a large church in Kansas City. He attended every major national church conference and seminar he possibly could. He was acutely aware of the need for vision and mission.

In fact, Jeff initiated a yearly planning retreat for his staff and key lay leadership. Yet he became increasingly frustrated at the lack of impact his church was making in the community.

On the long drive toward a retreat center for his third try at strategic planning, the chairman of his leadership team asked Jeff, "Pastor, why do this when no one ever follows through on the plans?"

This was an "Aha" moment for Jeff, as the remainder of the drive revolved around soul searching and intense examination. Plans are wonderful. Dreams are great. But with no follow-through and implementation, strategic disconnection will follow. It doesn't matter how good the strategy is if it's going to be ignored by the leadership team and the congregation.

The strategy may not be openly ignored, but there may be a more subtle lack of "forceful implementation." The result is the same.

Out of alignment!

3. The "Way We Were" Syndrome. Times change, defined targets change, and people change. But many churches don't change. Their best days are in the past. Their theme song is "Precious Memories." They remain committed to "the way we were" and haven't retooled their ministries to fit the new millennium.

Out of alignment!

4. Bipolar Disease. There's a lot of discussion today about what is called bipolar disease. It's a condition that causes a person to think one way at times and yet react in an entirely opposite way at other times. This condition is seen in church life as well. There are leaders who believe one way yet act in a completely contradictory way.

For example, a church task force in Houston was asked to come up with a plan to reach the teenagers in their community. The research was compiled, the legwork finished, and now it was time to present their findings to the church board. At the conclusion of their presentation, which included recommendations for a new youth music ministry, the task force sat at the table stunned as one of the board members declared, "Yes, we need to reach the youth, but we will not allow any drums in this church." Bipolar disease.

Out of alignment!

5. People Blindness. The Church cannot minister in today's world without being impacted by its culture. "People blindness" occurs when the Church fails to see the diversity of its surrounding culture—and the opportunity to minister to it.

Keith Phillips, president of World Impact, located in

downtown Los Angeles, has had a tremendous influence on the inner city. Because of his commitment to reach its diverse population, Christian schools and inner city clubs have been established that have brought a "Christian culture" to an environment that once was controlled by gangs.

Church planting is Keith's next step. He believes passionately that there is a need to plant inner-city, homogenous churches to provide a place of spiritual growth for those who have adopted this new Christian culture. Phillips ministers to 147 different people groups in the geographical area where his organization is located.

Almost every city has a similar area of ethnic diversity where a focused ministry could and should thrive. Hear the words of the Master: "Open your eyes and look at the fields! They are ripe for harvest (John 4:35).

It's time for alignment!

6. Dead Church Walking. In the film classic *Dead Man Walking*, the final days of death row inmates were portrayed. When a prisoner began his final walk to the execution chamber, prison guards would call out to the other prisoners, "Dead man walking!" so they could pay their last respects.

Unfortunately, thousands of "dead churches walking" exist. They have no mission, no strategy, no aggressive ministry planning. They are blind to the community's lost condition and its accompanying needs.

Jesus gave a warning to one of them, the church at Sardis (Rev. 3:1-3):

> To the angel of the church in Sardis write: These are the words of him who holds the seven spirits of God and the seven stars. I know your deeds; you have a reputation of being alive, but you are dead. Wake up! Strengthen what remains and is about to die, for I have not found your deeds complete in the sight of my God. Remember, therefore, what you have received and heard; obey it, and repent. But if you do not wake up, I

will come like a thief, and you will not know at what time I will come to you.

The ultimate misalignment: being out of God's will!

Attaining Vertical Alignment

You may remember an inexpensive childhood toy that was simply a framed, plastic-covered bald head on a small piece of painted cardboard. Inside the clear plastic were tiny iron strands. The object was to use an attached magnet wand to manipulate the iron fillings and create facial hair or a head of hair on the face.

The fillings would move and twitch as the small magnet was placed near them. Getting the iron fragments into place, into alignment, was initially difficult. But once they were in place, keeping them in alignment was rather easy.

Vertical alignment involves getting your ministry in place. It involves getting your vision directly from Christ and making sure the people can see it.

Vertical alignment is not
- The pastor preaching a message on the mission.
- The board telling the pastor, "OK—you do it!"
- The people cheering for the leaders, who are exhausted.

Vertical alignment is personally and intensely focusing on Christ and influencing everyone else to move in that same direction.

Keys to Vertical Alignment

There are four keys to making vertical alignment happen:

First, pray. On a very practical level, the ultimate expression of our desire for vertical alignment is in our praying for renewal. In the book *Your Pastor's Heart,* the authors advise pastors,

> We find, as do all our sheep, that it is a real battle to be able to pray properly. This battle, this spiritual war-

fare, is one of the most intense any pastor faces. Yet few recognize it as warfare. In fact, we are convinced that the spiritual warfare that surrounds prayer is more intense than that directed against evangelism. Those who know the power of prayer recognize that it is at the heart of everything God does on earth.[1]

**Prayer is the first thing, the second thing,
the third thing necessary to a minister.
Pray, then, my dear brother;
pray, pray, pray.**
—Edward Payson

Second, plan. Unfortunately, most North American churches are in a panic mode, trying to spin as many plates as they can without any of them falling and breaking. But effective churches plan! When a church has an established mission, all its plans and programs are aimed at that mission. Again, notice these planning stages:

Initial tactics are outlined to begin the process of goal setting.

Goals are vital to alignment. They help to measure "mission drift."

Next, stretch goals are unleashed. Pat Morley of *The Man in the Mirror*[2] calls his goals "BHAG's," Big Holy Audacious Goals—goals that are so great, only God could pull them off.

This leads to a five-year plan. Five-year segments appear to be the optimum length of time to work toward the target and to maintain momentum and measure progress.

Of course, this type of planning will take more than a one-day retreat. It's intensive *and* extensive!

Third, position. When the planning is finished, the people must be positioned and mobilized where they can best support the plans. However, this will happen only when the people understand the "what," "why," and "how" of these plans.

1. What are we trying to accomplish? What is the strategy? What is the long-term impact?

2. Why are these plans important to me? Why should I buy into them?

3. How do I fit into these plans? How will we pull them off?

Network,[3] a resource program from the Willow Creek Association, is a terrific plan for positioning people. People are positioned by their passion, spiritual gifts, and personal style, and Network has proven to be highly efficient in positioning people accordingly.

Fourth, promote. People need to be constantly reminded of their need for alignment. That principle should probably be promoted on a monthly basis—at least. The initial education will never be enough. Continuous monitoring and encouragement are vital for the successful implementation of any new ministry or change in ministry philosophy.

Keep talking about your plans. Keep celebrating the victories along the journey. Anticipate the ebb and flow of momentum, and build promotion into your planning.

Attaining Horizontal Alignment

Just as vertical alignment makes sure that the congregation is connected to the strategy, horizontal alignment links the church's activities with the target audience. There are four keys to horizontal alignment.

First, know your target. What are the needs and issues of the people in your community? Do you know the community's demographics? Who is your target audience?

George Hunter's *How to Reach Secular People* is both educational and compelling. Hunter's look into the secular world educates us to view our world with a secular world-view in order to reach the target audience. And he also compels us not to remain complacent in our efforts.

Dr. Hunter offers 10 characteristics of secular people. They are characteristics we must understand if we are to know our target audience.

1. Secular people are essentially ignorant of basic Christianity.
2. Secular people are seeking life *before* death.
3. Secular people are conscious of doubt more than guilt.
4. Secular people have a negative image of the Church.
5. Secular people have multiple alienations.
6. Secular people are untrusting.
7. Secular people have low self-esteem.
8. Secular people experience forces in history as "out of control."
9. Secular people experience forces in personality as "out of control."
10. Secular people cannot find "the door."[4]

Second, establish redundancy. The key to learning is repetition. Community Baptist Church did the research and has found that redundant classes are key to horizontal alignment. They offer each of their three classes four times each year and aggressively attempt to move the people through the process of alignment. The first is a membership class called "Getting Started" that's offered every three

---

As a community of worshipers

We have been sent into the world

To make, mature, and mobilize disciples

Who love the Lord our God above all else and

Who touch others with the reality of Jesus Christ

months and has functions to align people to the church's mission statement.

The church's goal is to educate the people concerning the importance of every ministry in the church moving toward this mission. So the three class sessions of this program are titled

Getting Started (Making Disciples)
Getting Grounded (Maturing Disciples)
Getting Connected (Mobilizing Disciples)

Each class is built on the prior one in order to present a continual process as shown below.

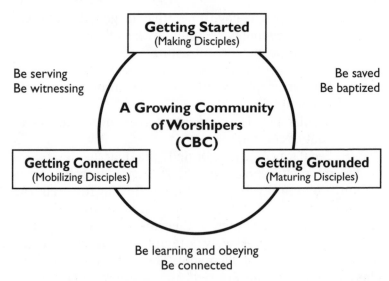

The second redundant class, which all graduates of "Getting Started" are expected to take, is called "Getting Grounded," whose purpose is to enable every church attender to understand the fundamental doctrines of the church. Most churches require new members to agree to their doctrinal statements, but have you ever wondered how many of these new people can understand what's included in a doctrinal treatise? An effective disciple both has a basic understanding of the tenets of his or her faith and is able to articulate them on the most basic levels.

The final redundant class is called "Getting Connected," which again aligns people to their responsibility in the Body. A nonserving believer is a contradiction. "Each one should use whatever gift he has received to serve others, faithfully administering God's grace in its various forms" (1 Pet. 4:10). An effective disciple-making church aggressively expects the people to plug in and discover how God can use them to advance His kingdom.

Since variety is one of the keys to effective church programming (without abandoning the core values), the diversity of redundant class offerings makes them invaluable to the overall health of the church.

Third, free up "second-curve" thinkers. In a previous chapter we discussed the five types of change seen in the Church. We suggested "transformational change" as the most effective. As "tactical change" is initiated, visionary leaders are casting vision and promoting the change. When this first curve is established, the visionary leader then passes the baton to those who will stabilize those ministries, while the leader continues the change process to the next level. This was the diagram offered:

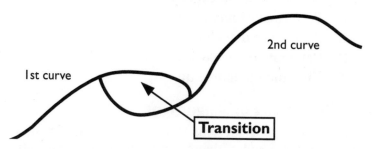

Once the first curve is stabilized, the leader becomes a "second-curve thinker." Second-curve thinkers are risk-takers. They enjoy thinking on the edge—and leading from the edge as well.

The church must learn to free these types of leaders from the mundane so they can continually plan the new ministry, the next target, or the next program that will need aligning down the road.

Fourth, measure progress. All too often, leadership teams begin the year "shooting arrows at the wall." Then they may conclude their year by drawing bull's-eyes around the arrows! True alignment isn't accomplished this way.

Establish the target first. In other words, begin the mission. Then identify "progress indicators."

Baptisms?	Sunday School attendance?
Decisions?	Attendance?
Lives changed?	Families healed?

What criteria will show that you've actually hit the target? What criteria will prove that the people and the programs are in alignment with the strategy of the church? Make sure that the entire leadership team understands and accepts both the indicators and the measuring process.

Remember: *do not expect what you choose not to inspect.*

I   **Initate respectful accountability.**

N   **Never confuse inspection with expectation.**

S   **Select what you expect.**

P   **Performance must be measurable.**

E   **Excellence demands it.**

C   **Celebrate the victories.**

T   **Take time to follow up.**[5]

Final Thoughts on Alignment

Alignment is a survival skill that you will constantly need to address and evaluate. No leader will be effective in pastoring in this new millennium without a clear sense of direction and the ability to stay on course.

Here are some final thoughts.

Help your leadership to think holistically. Reaching

the mission is not just the pastor's job. Reaching the lost is not just the evangelism committee's responsibility. Grounding new believers in the faith isn't just the job of the discipleship department. The mission is *everyone's* job.

Keep the mission before the people. You will never *oversell* the mission. Everyone in the church should be able to articulate the church's mission. When you think the people have finally understood, tell them one more time.

Acknowledge and reward "mission workers." Who are the heroes in your church? Typically we clap and cheer for our heroes. "Fred and Ethel" host a potluck—we give them a round of applause for their efforts. "Ricky and Lucy" re-do the bulletin boards—we recognize their talents. When was the last time you cheered for someone who invited an unbeliever to church? When was the last time you clapped for a prayer warrior? Think mission!

Be ruthless in the reviewing process. It's true—we're talking church, but let's be honest about how we're doing. If a ministry is in alignment with the will of God and the energy of the people, something will happen. Positive change will take place. But if the horse dies—dismount. Why ride a dying program that's out of alignment with the overall mission?

Realize that the mission never changes. Good leaders understand that "the main thing" must remain "the main thing." When approached about *the main thing* one day, Jesus was asked, "So what is the greatest commandment?" With lawyer-like finesse, our Lord answered, "'Love the Lord your God with all your heart and with all your soul and with all your mind.' This is the first and greatest commandment. And the second is like it: 'Love your neighbor as yourself'" (Matt. 22:37-39).

The effective new millennium leader also recognizes that changes are required if the organization is to hit its target. Since the target is continually moving, the programming must be adjusted to hit the target!

But the "mission" is the plumb line to keep us on track —and it must never change.

Keep praying. Is your church a threat to the devil? Most churches aren't! Leaving church late one night, Glen saw a man across the parking lot sitting in front of a candle. Noticing Glen, he stood to his feet and screamed, "Satan!"

Glen said, "I smiled and got in my car, and decided to drive by and see if I recognized this person. He walked alongside my car yelling the same thing over and over as I drove away. I immediately did two things. I first prayed a hedge of protection around my family, because every leader who is advancing the cause of Christ not only has a bulls-eye on their back but also on the back of their family members. Second, I praised God all the way home."

If Satan had sent this person to pray against our church, we must be doing something right, he thought.

If your church is threatening the enemy, you might as well get ready for some opposition!

Leader, you're in the cockpit. Alignment is vital to your safe landing in ministry. Indeed, it is a survival skill to consider in your preflight checkout.

Are you confident in your destination? Is your crew, your leadership team, on board?

Are you educated in the measurement instrumentation God has provided to keep you on course?

Have you shared your flight plan with the rest of the passengers? Do you have key people in place to implement it, those who are sold on the mission?

Alignment affords confidence in the destination, in your crew, and in the Divine Pilot, who promises to get you there safely!

Now pull back on the throttle and have a great flight!

7

TEAM SKILLS

A SAILOR ONCE TOOK A MAN FISHING who loved the land and hated the water. The old gentlemen didn't know how to swim and knew nothing about fishing. Later in the afternoon, after an uneventful day on the water, the fellow hooked a fish that was so large it bent the fishing pole over. It was the kind of catch every fisherman dreams of.

The huge fish was relentless in its attempt to escape, jumping from the water and pulling on the line. As he reeled in his catch, the landlubber got excited about his prize. In his enthusiasm he leaned too far over the boat and fell into the water. Panic-stricken, he began to call out, "Help! Save me!" "Help! Save me!"

The veteran sailor calmly reached out and grabbed the man by the hair of his head. But as he pulled, the man's toupee came off, and he slipped under the water once again. In a few seconds the man surfaced, screaming, "Help! Save me!" The sailor leaned over the side of the boat and yelled, "How can I help you if you won't stick together?"

Teamwork is about sticking together! Team skills are a vital skill for ministry in the new millennium.

The Benefits of Teamwork

It has been said that individuals sign autographs, individuals endorse products, and individuals grant interviews, but *teams* win championships. In the Church we have much more at stake than a championship. The eternal destiny of human souls is on the line.

Glenn M. Parker is the president of a consulting firm based in Lawrenceville, New Jersey, that specializes in human resource and organizational development. In his book *Team Players and Teamwork*[1], he discusses the value of working as a team. From a survey of 51 companies Parker was able to rank the ways that teamwork contributes to the success of a business.

Benefits	Rank
Greater productivity	1
Effective use of resources	1
Better problem solving	1
Better quality products and services	2
Creativity and innovation	3
Higher-quality decisions	3[2]

Despite the fact that the book was written from a secular point of view, it speaks to pastors about the need for greater skill at problem solving and decision-making in the Church. Reaching our postmodern audience for Christ will require great innovation, creativity, and service. As George Cladis notes,

> After twenty years of ministry involving a lot of trial and error, I have come to a rock-solid conviction that has revolutionized my ministry: if a church is to succeed in carrying out a healthy ministry and developing a good Christian community, there must be stable and high-quality relationships among the members of the principle leadership team. . . . Team-based ministry is the most effective model for leading and organizing Christian ministry for the twenty-first century.[3]

Ministry action teams offer many advantages to the church. Those advantages become more critical as a local church goes through various stages of growth. The larger a church becomes, the more difficulty it will have in developing the "family" feel of the smaller church.

Thus, one of the paradoxes of church growth is the need to grow larger and smaller simultaneously. Smaller ministry teams are better able to meet the needs of a large congregation. And the pressure brought on by the furious rate of change in our world has created a renewed desire among people to serve in ministry as members of a team.

Cladis goes on to introduce seven team-based leadership models that will have lasting value. They will have a great impact on leadership style in the new millennium.[4]

A Team Definition

A very simple definition of a team is a group of people who have gathered together—united in purpose, complementary in skills, supportive in communication—with a passion to fulfill their God-given mission with urgency and accountability.

Let's take a closer look at this definition. First, a team is a group of people with a united purpose. They are driven with an overriding purpose to succeed in the responsibility they have been assigned or called to accomplish. They will therefore help out in every area for the cause of the team.

Second, a team will complement one another with their gift mix and talents. For the Church to function properly, every gift must function, and every gift must be deemed important. Paul wrote, "Now the body is not made up of one part but of many. If the foot should say, 'Because I am not a hand, I do not belong to the body,' it would not for that reason cease to be part of the body" (1 Cor. 12:14-15). He then goes on to say how the eye and ear each have their importance and how God has arranged all the parts to function as a unit. This is the complementary nature of the team. Bobb Biehl says, "No dream, no team."[5]

Third, a team will be a group who communicate well. In other words, they talk to one another. They may have to say some very tough things, but that's how a team functions openly. Their body language and tone of speech is monitored carefully because a lot is at stake—the team!

Fourth, a team seeks to accomplish their task with urgency and accountability. When life is in the balance and eternity is at stake for family and friends for the Kingdom of God, teams get serious. Yes, they will have fun together. Yes, they have their lighter moments. But a team will not back down from responsibilities and opportunities.

This definition of teamwork is easily identified in the New Testament. Paul and Barnabas functioned as a team to choose the elders of the local churches they planted. Paul teamed up with Timothy when they sent a letter to Philippi, which included the elders, deacons, and people at large in the church (Phil. 1:1). Elders functioned as teams as they were challenged by Peter to shepherd the people of God (1 Pet. 5:1-5). Deacons functioned as teams in caring for the Hellenistic widows of Acts 6. Teams were everywhere in New Testament days, and teams remain a vital part of the organization for ministry in this new millennium.

Setting the Stage for Teams

Phil Jackson's ability as a basketball coach is unparalleled. At the dawn of a new century, he used the age-old concept of teamwork to win yet another National Basketball Association championship, this time with the Los Angeles Lakers. As coach, Jackson identified the role and responsibilities of each player. Nearly all his players made a direct contribution to winning the championship.

Using Jackson's team model, a leader must first consider the individual strengths and weakness of the team and its members. What kind of team will be most useful in achieving the purpose of the organization? Here are seven team models to choose from.

Task Force. A task force is a team designed to complete a particular task or to solve a particular problem, and then disbands. One church in Texas embraced the use of task forces and moved away from standing committees. A church leader remarked, "It got to the point where the committees had to meet about nothing, and that's what we ended up doing—nothing."

Committees naturally become stagnant when they're given nothing important to do. A task force can be assembled to address specific issues such as a parking problem, Sunday School overcrowding, or to choose the discipleship curriculum for the coming year. When the parking problem has been resolved, for example, there's no more need for that task force to meet.

Specialized Team. Some ministry tasks require the expertise of people who are competent in a certain field. A small Lutheran church in Ohio found the need for a specialized team to go beyond the work of a task force. When the church opened an elementary school, a special task force was assigned to do the planning. But the task force failed to establish plans for the next level of Christian education. A specialized ministry team composed of professional educators was then formed.

The specialized team set about to earn accreditation for the school, a monumental task that required long-term commitment and buy-in by the team. They revised the pay scale for teachers and established a plan for their continuing education and ongoing salary adjustments. The specialized team accomplished much more than the task force, but it also required a longer time frame of commitment.

Leadership Team. The pastoral staff and the governing board compose the leadership team in most churches. Leadership teams are, by their very nature, hierarchical, because someone must be at the helm to steer the ship. This team also functions as the command team for the church, assigning responsibilities to other teams and receiving feedback from them. The leadership team uses that interaction to evaluate the ministry of the church and to determine what improvements are needed to move the church to the next level of ministry.

These first three types of teams are more formal. They

are elected or hand picked to guide a particular project or an entire parish ministry. The next two are informal teams, which tend to be more spontaneous and are often loosely structured.

Mentoring Team. The title sounds formal, but the team assignment is not. Often mentoring teams simply meet informally once a week to discuss one facet of the ministry. For example, no formal meeting may be called, but a few workers in the children's program may get together for coffee or an informal lunch to discuss the best way to deal with a troubled child.

For example, Pat Morley's organization Man in the Mirror has a goal to get men into informal teams like those following a catalytic event so they can grow and learn together. These teams might also be called small groups, discipleship groups, or mentoring groups.

Ad Hoc Team. Ad hoc teams are similar to the task force team, but they usually have less authority. They're investigative teams assembled to address an immediate issue. For example, an ad hoc team might be assembled to review sound equipment resources and make recommendations to the board of deacons. They are typically composed of people who have demonstrated a knowledge for a particular ministry area.

Another team category is the self-managed team. These teams demonstrate many attributes of both the formal and informal teams. Here are some examples:

High-Performance Team. High-performance teams are specialized and spontaneous. A church in Washington has a high-performance worship team. They meet informally as a creative team to design the upcoming worship service.

This type of team needs the freedom to create and experiment. The Church as a whole was designed by God to be a high-performance team. "God created the church, with its various parts or gifts, to work together to achieve excellence just as the various parts of the gymnast's body do.

Paul declares that though we are many parts, we are one body (1 Corinthians 12).[6]" We are the Body of Christ, a high-performance team.

Cross-training Team. These teams cover a variety of areas where weaknesses have been discovered. Cross-training teams are empowered to make decisions "on the fly" where a delay in the decision-making process would inhibit ministry. They have a firm grasp of the overall ministry.

Ingredients of Effective Teams

We, like many baby boomers, are playing a little catch-up when it comes to our retirement programs. But what we soon learn with all the data collected in the financial pilgrimage is the value of investments. Long-term investments will pay off when given ample time to mature.

Investing in a team also pays long-term benefits. Your ultimate success in this new millennium of ministry is not conditional on building capacity and programming expertise. Your success will rest upon your ability and desire to invest in other teammates.

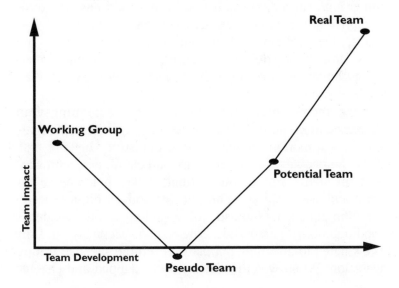

Here are five essentials for developing your dream team in ministry:

First, learn the art of *delegation.* Delegation is just that—an art. We have found most pastors afraid of delegation and thus find themselves on the ministry treadmill praying they don't get "voted off the island." Delegation begins with stating desired results and helping the team process through these expectations. This is not the place to stress methods. Stress the results, the mission and vision of your church. Perry Smith in his *Rules and Tools for Leaders* shares, "An essential element of the . . . delegation process is making sure that associates understand the organizational values, goals, priorities, and the 'big picture.'"[7] Delegation then moves to written goals and timelines. If your goals have not yet passed through your fingertips, they are probably not focused. And if your goals have no concluding date, they have little urgency. Next, delegation demands shared authority. How much freedom will you allow? When will updates and reports be due? Much of the frustration of delegation can be managed most effectively when appropriate ground rules are established in the beginning. Once the responsibilities have been assigned and buy-in has taken place, the final stage of delegation is the evaluation process. How did we do? Did we accomplish everything we set out to finish? All successful teams learn and practice the art of delegation.

The second essential ingredient in developing your dream team in ministry is *empowerment.* Question: Who are the most important people in your ministry? They are typically the people you clap for. The potluck dinner is finished and the moderator of the potluck makes her way to the front and asks boldly, "Who put this potluck dinner together? Who did such a fantastic job at getting all this wonderful food organized?" Fred and Barney come sheepishly out from the kitchen to a standing applause from the satisfied troops. Question: When was the last time you clapped and cheered for a prayer warrior in your church? How about a "standing-O" for those people who regularly invite their unsaved friends to church? Are potluck dinners important? Sure, but nowhere near the importance in the grand scale of eternity as those other two activities within the Body of Christ. So cheer for them. Your affirmation empowers them to greater activity. This empowerment in a team gives permission to use their gifts and talents with enthusiasm and passion. Perry Smith writes, "A good leader spends a considerable amount of time complimenting and thanking people who work for him or her. Indeed, it is quite an art to do this in a way that conveys sincerity, compliments people who should be complimented, and subtly leaves out the few people who do not deserve to be commended."[8]

The third ingredient is *support*. Every teammate wants to work with people who will both encourage them and support them in the journey. We have found when people are trained and commissioned with little support, they will often complete a task but will lack desire to sign on for future responsibility. When a person is trained and becomes part of an exciting team, ministry becomes a lifestyle. Become a cheerleader and a coach. Direct the team and support the accomplishments.

The fourth ingredient is *motivation*. Everyone is motivated a little differently. Some are motivated financially. Others are motivated by recognition. But most, if thought through deeply as a Christian, will tell you that the greatest motivation in their life is an eternal motivation. Paul wrote in 2 Cor. 4:16-18, "Therefore we do not lose heart. Though outwardly we are wasting away, yet inwardly we are being renewed day by day. For our light and momentary troubles are achieving for us an eternal glory that far outweighs them all. So we fix our eyes not on what is seen, but on what is unseen. For what is seen is temporary, but what is unseen is eternal." Most of us don't like to put it quite that bluntly. But it's the truth—our bodies are wasting away. If you doubt this truth, look in the mirror. You're wasting away! A representative for handicapped people once said this: "There are three types of people in the world: Those who are born with handicaps; those who have developed handicaps through injury or aging; and those who are temporarily living in healthy bodies."[9] This is why an eternal perspective is vital in life and in teams. But know this—effective teams have leadership motivating them. Motivation is allowing others to catch your passion and get excited about being involved.

QUALITIES OF EXCEPTIONAL PASTOR-COACHES

They accept others.
They are flexible.
They enjoy challenges.
They are self-aware.
They value giftedness in others.
They are courageous.
They are supportive of others.
They keep agreements.
They share information freely.
They are filled with the Holy Spirit.
They listen.
They facilitate others.
They understand group dynamics.
They understand process improvement.
They know how to manage meetings.
They know how to manage projects.
They give feedback.
They can let go of personal agendas.
They resolve conflicts.
They are good communicators. [10]

The last ingredient is *evaluation.* How did we do? What did we really accomplish? This can be an annual event or a monthly activity. Evaluation can be written or verbal. Evaluation is merely the measurement of what got done and how effective this ministry has been and resources have been used. Your responsibility in this process of evaluation is "speaking the truth in love" (Eph. 4:15). Share the facts—lovingly. Give the details—lovingly. But do share the facts and give the details.

8

ENDURANCE SKILLS

THE STORY IS TOLD OF A LADY who wanted a pet. She decided to buy a German shepherd because she had heard how easy this breed of dog was to train. To her dismay, after a couple of months the dog still wasn't trained. It seemed that her every command was ignored. So she enrolled her new pet in the "Kute K-9 Dog Obedience School."

After a few short weeks of training, the dog was brought home. And sure enough, it had been thoroughly trained. It had learned every voice command in the dog training manual. There was a slight problem, however. The new owner had named her dog "Stay." The poor mutt nearly lost its mind when she tried to call it to dinner: "Come, Stay!"

Too many commands?

Too much survival training?

You don't know what to do next?

Preparing for new millennial ministry can be a bit overwhelming. The threat of impossible expectations, unbelievable uncertainties, relentless responsibilities, and plenty of stress!

One pastor recently estimated that 80 percent of the clergy in his denomination have thought about giving up the ministry at sometime in the past month. Whether that number is realistic or not, the fact is, many pastors *are* ready to quit. The stress symptoms are many.

Some suffer insomnia.

Others eat too much.

Some indulge in secret addictive behavior.

So who cares? Nobody pastors the pastor. Everyone can tell you a crash-and-burn story about somebody in the ministry. The pressures of ministry will only escalate in this new century and millennium. It's important that pastors be able to take care of the most vital person in their families and churches—themselves.

There's no quick fix. The lone survivor on that first *Survivor Island* television episode walked away with the prize because he endured until the very end. Snakes, rats, thunderstorms, conniving and criticizing associates wouldn't deter him.

Modern ministry survivors will need that kind of tenacity.

Survival will take every ounce of commitment. Here are a few steps that will certainly help:

1. Get a handle on stress.

From the beginning of time, stress has been a part of the life experience. Adam and Eve experienced the first stress. One day after a lunch appointment had turned into a fiasco, God (their Boss) called them to an emergency meeting. It was a very stressful situation, to say the least. First, there was stress about what to wear to the meeting. And second, they didn't know how the Board of Heaven would react to the fiasco. As an added pressure, the rumors of a sudden transfer had been hanging over their heads ever since that lunch! And since some of the previous inhabitants had crawled away, they had also heard about staff cutbacks at Garden of Eden, Inc.

Stress levels haven't changed much since then. But the way we think about that stress, as well as the way we cope with it, has undergone a few modifications in these days. Some of the old stress relievers are as obsolete as a hat pin. In days of yore, the family came home from work or school and sat in front of the television set with a *Swanson* TV dinner on their TV tray. With the flick of a wrist (no remote control), one channel switch could transport the "stress-ees" to a happy *Ozzie and Harriet* land, where all of life's woes were solved in 30 minutes (including time for the commercials).

It's a new day. These days getting the family together in one place at the same time is a miracle nigh unto the parting of the Red Sea. Stragglers coming and going to the family room struggle for authority over the remote control—or bicker over the use of the TV screen itself. Some want to watch "professional" wrestling, while others want to play a Nintendo game.

The only constant is the TV dinner. (But even that has changed since the introduction of the new microwaveable edition.)

Modern families have discovered that office or school stress is transferable. It's brought home like an unused sack lunch. And pastors are not excluded from the problem!

Our attitude toward stress is important. We used to think that stress was an enemy to be avoided at all costs. We now know that stress cannot be avoided. And it probably won't go away until the trumpet sounds.

Understand the positive side of stress. We can actually be on friendly terms with stress if we determine to *use it* instead of letting *it use us*. For example, the dynamics of stress can help to surface and solve a problem that has been previously hidden. It can be illustrated like this: When we suffer a sprain, the physical pain is a surface indicator of the hidden physical injury. Likewise, a stressful situation is a surface reminder of a hidden anxiety (either personal or relational) that needs to be dealt with.

Understand the stress points. There was a little girl whose daddy was living in the fast lane. He hurried here and there, necktie loosened, and always brought home a briefcase bulging with papers. One day the little girl inquired, "Why does daddy always bring home all those papers?"

Her mother replied, "Daddy has so much work to do that he can't finish it all at the office. That's why he brings it home at night."

The girl was perplexed. She turned to her father and asked, "Daddy, if you're having trouble getting your work done, why don't they put you in a slower group?"

Great question! There are moments in every pastor's life when he or she longs to be placed in the slower group. But there isn't one!

All church ministries are stressful! The problems may be modified slightly by size, but all leaders deal with the same basic pressures, problems, and insecurities. For instance, all pastors face high expectations—the continual demand to do more and achieve more. The size of the church does not alter that fact. The misconception is that a larger church has more volunteers, and thus the stress load on the pastor is smaller. In actuality, stress is stress, no matter whether the pastor is leading 1 or 1,000.

Factor	Intensity	Frequency/ Duration	Total
	5—painful 3—headaches 1—everyday stuff	5—never lets up 3—half the time 1—almost never	
1. Change/threat of transfer			
2. Overload, too much work			
3. Conflicting vision			
4. Conflict with people			
5. Personal habits			
6. Lack of support			
7. Leadership stress			
8. Financial problems			
9. Unfair expectations			
10. Lack of balance between home and church			

There are common pressure points (stress points) in pastoral ministry. The preceeding examination will help to evaluate the stress faced by a pastor. Rank each stress from 1 to 5, with 5 meaning high stress and 1 meaning low stress.

Pastors rarely score below 50 on this evaluative tool, which indicates consistently high levels of stress and pain. Most of these leaders are already familiar with the sentiments expressed by the psalmist: "The sacrifices of God are a broken spirit; a broken and contrite heart" (Ps. 51:17).

"Been there, done that, and bought the T-shirt!"

And thankfully, some of those same leaders have felt the balm of Jesus' promise "Take my yoke upon you and learn from me, for I am gentle and humble in heart, and you will find rest for your souls" (Matt. 11:29). But modern ministry is simply overwhelming at times. There are days when it seems like all of the stress points have worked their way into our daily journal.

Learn to handle the stress points. Let's take a look at these ministry stress points and learn the skills that will help us increase our endurance in ministry.

• **Change of assignment or the threat of transfer.** In an ideal world, the minister unpacks the U-Haul, stacks the books on the office shelves, takes the lid off the "sermon barrel," and looks forward to the retirement party! But in the real world, ministry assignments often change. Evolving ministry philosophies and demographics almost certainly affect the tenure of the pastoral staff.

What skills need to be developed to face assignment change, or to transfer stress? First, don't plan for them! We serve where we serve *on purpose*. It's not a temporary rung on our career ladder. It's a harvest field. And the Lord of the Harvest has placed us where He needs us. Plan to stay awhile.

Second, if a change of assignment or transfer is on the horizon, praise the Lord for it! It means that you've completed that assignment and have been found trustworthy enough to go on to another.

Third, don't take it personally. Everyone in ministry has *those days*, *those weeks*, *those months*, *those years* that he or she would like to repeat, like a high school typing class. But time can't be turned back. You did the best you could. Stan Toler remembers being in Washington, D.C., when President Reagan addressed the returning Iranian hostages following the 1980s crisis. He gave them some good advice when he said, "Turn the page." In other words, leave the pain and suffering behind. Simply go on.

• **Overload.** Overload is dangerous, because it increases our deficiencies while it reduces our defenses. A minister living on the edge is more susceptible to falling. Jesus said, "Simply let your 'Yes' be 'Yes,' and your 'No,' 'No'; anything beyond this comes from the evil one" (Matt. 5:37). Why is it that in the ministry language, a "Yes" is easier to enunciate than a "No?"

Well-known Southern Baptist preacher Adrian Rogers was asked by a Christian television interviewer why burnout is so common. He replied, "Because some pastors are burning wick and not oil." What profound truth! If the Lord's not in it, leave it alone! God won't lead His followers off the cliff. A *first-thing-in-the-morning* search for God's anointing and leading instead of our own planning and scheming will help to cure the overload syndrome.

Also, learn to share the load. Helping others discover what God has given them to share in Kingdom-building, and then releasing them to do it, can alleviate the problem of overload.

• **Conflicting vision.** Stan had a pastor friend who didn't survive. His attitude was "my way or the highway," which is a dangerous philosophy for modern ministry. There will be times when the people's vision differs from the pastor's. For example, when a church changes to a "multitrack" approach to ministry, problems will likely result. As we've seen, any changes in philosophy or program can be met with stubborn resistance. And going from *two blended services* to *two dis-*

tinctly different types of services represents a major shift in thinking for most churches.

People's fears will swarm like picnic flies on a pumpkin pie in comments like "We won't know everyone" or "All the young couples are going to go to the contemporary service, and we won't see them anymore." There will also be headaches caused by the pressure on housekeeping, parking, and personnel.

Realistically, when we've done our job in helping people think for themselves, there will be times when their thinking will differ from ours. What happens when there's a collision? First, understand that ministers don't have a corner on the "vision market." The Bible advises us that there is wisdom in *many* counselors. God may be speaking through that very person whose opinion you're ignoring. Second, thank the Lord that your vision teaching has "caught," and build from the principles you share in common with the congregation's version.

● **Conflict with people.** If it weren't for people in our congregations, the stress level would be much lower. Think of how ridiculous that sounds. Our ministry is all about people—stubborn people, sweet people, critical people, kind people, talented people, bumbling people. People for whom God sacrificed His Son.

Without them, our churches would be rather empty. But as surely as we have varieties of people, we have varieties of *people problems*. We knew that even before we knelt at the ordination altar.

In fact, we already knew a lot of "those" people—and probably lived with some—before we went into the ministry. The minister who hasn't learned to work with people will suffer extreme stress.

What kind of people skills does the new millennium pastor need? For sure, they will need to *love people*. People need to know someone cares about them. They live in a cold, impersonal world. They live in a world of answering machines and telemarketers who can't pronounce their names. They need a personal word of encouragement from someone who really cares about them.

Second, people need to be *confronted without getting into a confrontation*. There are some folks who can flat out tell us off without making us mad. How did they do it? They probably sandwiched their criticism between compliments, for one thing. They probably worked hard not to raise their voice. They probably smiled or gave a reassuring handshake or hug. They probably let us know that we're really worth something before they approached that area of conflict.

They probably acted like Jesus!

• **Personal habits.** Personal habits can easily get out of control and become not only stress points but also issues of character or integrity. Here are three observations about leaders and credibility. First, leaders usually have greater strengths than weaknesses, but still they have weaknesses.

Second, leaders are on the front line of spiritual warfare, highly susceptible to Satan's attack, usually among the first victims of spiritual battles. If Satan can get to the leaders, he can get to the followers.

Third, leaders must live by a higher standard than their followers. In Luke 12:48 Jesus said, "From everyone who has been given much, much will be demanded; and from the one who has been entrusted with much, much more will be asked." James 3:1 states, "Not many of you should presume to be teachers, my brothers, because you know that we who teach will be judged more strictly."

Skills? We're in a helping profession, yet our own needs often go unmet. We must learn to do for ourselves what we do for others. Here are some tips on self-nurture.

Get enough rest. Many pastors don't. Especially in a growing church, we face the very real temptation to burn the candle at both ends. We run from the office to the committee meeting and then to the Bible study. Twelve-hour days and 60-hour weeks are not uncommon in the ministry.

For some pastors they're the norm. Stop it! God made us as fragile beings. Learn to say "no." Get some rest.

Diet and exercise properly. Ten thousand doctors can't be wrong. We feel better and are healthier when we respect our bodies.

Take time off. Many pastors feel guilty when they relax. Don't. Most laypersons enjoy that most wonderful of modern creations every week—the weekend. Pastors must force themselves and their churches to accept the fact that their schedule is abnormal. They need permission (sometimes from themselves) to take a day off in the middle of the week. Put it in the datebook—then do it.

Develop close friendships. Isolation is common in the pastorate. Pastors are often separated from their extended family members. Their social lives are usually limited to interaction with parishioners. It may take some effort, but identify a friend and build a relationship. Isolation is dangerous. Reach out and touch someone.

Pursue a hobby. Fly fishing. Woodworking. Golf. Tennis. Camping. Photography. Every pastor should find something other than work to occupy a portion of his or her time. It will free the mind, ease stress, and provide a sense of achievement.

Maintain a devotional life. Pastors pray for a living, but they must also pray to survive. It's disgustingly easy for a pastor to fall into the trap of being a "professional Christian." A pastor must make the effort to build personal spiritual disciplines into his or her life. Here are a few:

Prayer. Nobody ever thinks that he or she prays enough, and probably that's right. But regular prayer, even for a brief time, is important. The length of one's prayer is far less important than the *habit* of prayer.

Scripture. The pastor who reads the Word only to find sermon material will be just as dry spiritually as he or she is in the pulpit. The Bible is not only our source of spiritual strength—it's also the greatest literature in the world. The pastor who drinks deeply from the well of Scripture will be spiritually healthy.

Reflection. Pastors get paid to talk—and sometimes they want to be quiet! Practice the discipline of silence occasionally. Spend time pondering Scripture. This is different than prayer. Reflection is the art of thinking deeply, spiritually, theologically. The pastor who spends time in silence will likely have something worth hearing when he or she decides to speak.

Retreat. It's important to take some time away from the regular routine for prayer, study, and reflection. Even a day alone with God is useful. Many pastors plan two- to three-day retreats into their schedule a couple of times a year. These days of "doing nothing" will make any pastor much more productive.

Journal. For centuries, many Christians have found a spiritual value in keeping a journal. Writing in a journal is a variation on reflection. It facilitates self-examination and offers a record of spiritual progress that may later be useful personally or professionally.

● **Lack of support.** "It's lonely at the top," the old saying goes. It's especially lonely if it feels as though no one's looking up to you. What do you do if you're a leader and no one seems to be following? Don't panic. Remember the scene at Calvary? Only Jesus' mother and one or two other followers stood by. Everyone else had left the Savior. Leadership is lonely at times.

But what if the lack of a crowd results from their disagreement with you? Again, don't panic. Stay the course. Keep the focus on the mission. Align the team and wait it out. Just as *leading* is a process, so is *following*. The support will come—and sometimes it comes long after your tenure is over.

In the meantime, be sure the troops understand the battle plan. How's the communication? Are the assignments plain and simple? Have you put expectations on someone who really isn't gifted in that area? The checklist is a good survivalist survey.

● **Leadership stress.** This stress point is the opposite of lack of support. Leadership stress comes from too much success. It's like being Tiger Woods in a miniature golf tournament. Can you imagine the pressure of the expectation? Maybe you can—on a smaller scale. Nobody but the person who's been there understands what it's like to stand before the local church or the board and be expected to deliver eternal answers to life questions.

The cure is quite simple. Trust the Lord. Now, before you say that advice sounds a little too trite to you, remember what the Master said: "When you are brought before synagogues, rulers and authorities, do not worry about how you will defend yourselves or what you will say, for the Holy Spirit will teach you at that time what you should say" (Luke 12:11-12). The common ministry assignments are all there: "synagogues," "rulers," and "authorities." Sounds like a church service, a district gathering, and a board meeting, doesn't it? It's not just an end-times prophecy. It's a *these-times* prophecy. God isn't surprised by new-millennium ministry pressures.

Remember—He wouldn't have called you if He hadn't intended to equip you.

● **Financial problems.** Talk about stress! If you're a pastor, you know what it's like to have only enough money for two pieces of a three-piece suit. You probably didn't enter the ministry for money—and you probably haven't been disappointed either! The stress of "more month than money" is relentless.

What financial survival skills will you need? *Keep it simple.* It's a timeless financial principle. You've probably been taught from early childhood to "live within your means." But some of that childhood truth seems to get lost in the translation. Here's an updated version: "Live within your means." Not everything that looks good is good for you.

A hundred good sermons can be washed away in a sea of debt!

The words of Wesley still ring true: "Earn all you can, save all you can, give all you can." It's still a good financial plan. Some promising ministries have been abandoned because the "earning" was more important than the "saving" and the "giving."

● **Unfair expectations.** Preachers used to worry about how their ministries compared to the Swaggerts, Humbards, Bakers, or Schullers. With the exception of Dr. Robert Schuller, they've all dropped off the radar screen.

Still, every pastor whose parishioner has given him or her a report about that "great crusade evangelist" they just heard knows what the pressure of comparison can do to the stress level. Maybe you just completed a 13-week study of the Gospel of Matthew, but sure as the world, one of your parishioners will visit some church on their vacation and come back with the question "Pastor, have you ever thought of preaching an expository series?" Stress.

What do you do? First, remember who called you. You're just a corporal. Jesus is the Captain. You're one of the troops, and the Captain has promised to arm the soldiers for battle. Second, be kind to that "reporter." He or she is well-meaning. Third, communicate better. When you're making a significant contribution of sermon time and preparation, build it up in the church publications. We ought to be more excited about sharing the Bread of Life than a Kroger store is about sharing day-old whole wheat!

● **Lack of balance between home and church.** Cosmetics mogul Mary Kay said that her life was ordered on these priorities: God first, family second, business third. For the pastor, that puts church at the bottom of the list. It sounds wrong, but it's right. Personal spirituality and family responsibility must come before career. A pastor who accepts that priority will sleep better and most likely will be less stressed out.

Put your spouse and your kids on the calendar. Surely, time with them is more important than that study committee for the purchase of sidewalk salt for the winter season!

2. Work on your personal development.

Howard Hendricks said that if you stop learning today, you stop teaching tomorrow. He's right. Consider yourself a student, not only of Jesus Christ but also the world. Make the decision that you'll not be satisfied with ignorance. Let's reiterate.

Read constantly. Books, magazines, journals. A wise pastor will read everything he or she can lay his or her hands on.

Acquire computer skills. Welcome to the 21st century. Technology is here to stay. A pastor who can use common software programs such as word processing, spreadsheet, and presentation design applications will double productivity and discover new ministry possibilities.

Pursue educational opportunities. Develop educational goals, and pursue them. As we've already said, continuing education is a possibility for many pastors. And opportunities for more formal training also abound. For instance, doctor of ministry programs are increasingly accessible and affordable. Other opportunities such as seminars and workshops should be a consistent feature of any pastor's routine.

Travel. International travel has tremendous educational and self-development value. Creative planning and careful budgeting may be required, but a trip to Israel or Europe may not be as far-fetched as it sounds. Miniterm missions are also excellent self-development tools.

Network. Meet with other clergy when possible. Comparing notes, swapping ideas, and just plain crying on a colleague's shoulder are all helpful at times. Develop a "gospel clique" of like-minded pastors to test your ideas on. Collegial relationships are a must.

Invite feedback. It's a challenge for the fragile ego, but the best way to discover areas for growth is by inviting feedback. Ask a trusted parishioner to critique a sermon. Invite a colleague to evaluate ministry strengths and weaknesses. Listen to what friends say, both positive and negative. Use that feedback to identify skills that need refinement.

3. Guard your ministry.

Not only are pastors not immune from temptation— there are some ways in which we seem even more vulnerable to Satan's attacks. The pressure on ministers and their families won't decrease in this new century and millennium. Every pastor must learn to practice the art of spiritual self-defense.

Self-define. Again, pastoral expectations have exploded in the past decade. Churches expect more from their pastors, and most pastors expect more from themselves. The pressure to perform is stressful at best, punishing at worst. The pastor who survives those escalating pressures will be the one who has a clear-cut job description and has laypersons who understand.

Self-examine. The traditional advice to a young minister on dealing with sexual temptation goes something like this: "Never counsel a woman alone." That nostrum implies that sexual attraction is an irresistible force that might attack the unwary male pastor by surprise. Once alone in the presence of a woman, he would be helpless to resist. In reality this, like any other temptation, has more to do with the inside than the outside. In other words, it's the pastor's heart condition, rather than the attractiveness of the opposite sex, that creates the temptation. Better advice to the novice pastor would be this: Admit it when you are lonely, or tell someone when you feel like a failure. Being honest (even with oneself) about issues such as rejection, loneliness, or inadequacy is a vital skill for survival in a highly pressurized vocation.

Self-discipline. Most people have one or two glaring weaknesses. Very few people seem to be weak in all areas. Some of us seem genetically prone to use addictive substances like alcohol. Others have no problem with alcohol but will lie or steal if necessary to acquire money. Wise people, and certainly wise pastors, have an understanding of their own psyche. They know what makes them tick. They know what tempts them. And they avoid them.

Self-report. It's not new advice, but it's still good. Get an accountability partner. Find someone you can trust, and give that person permission to ask anything. Here are some good accountability questions:

Is there any unconfessed sin in your life?

What is your greatest area of spiritual struggle right now?

What do you think you need to do in order to avoid sin in that area?

Have you prayed since we last met?

We Win!

In the final analysis, the survivor child of God will never lose. Calvary made that person a winner. Even when the last breath of ministry life has escaped from the sagging lungs of its owner, the breath of heaven will invade it with eternity.

Until we see Christ face to face, stay focused on God's mission. Stay true to yourself and those you love. Brace yourself for the taunts and temptations of the enemy. And get ready for a celestial homecoming beyond your wildest dreams!

Survival isn't a method. It's a state of mind embedded by the One who turned a cemetery into a celebration!

Notes

Chapter 1

1. George Barna, "The State of the Church" (Barna Research Online; available on-line at < http://barna.org > 21 March 2000).

2. Mike Regele, *The Death of the Church* (Grand Rapids: Zondervan Publishing House, 1995), 19.

3. George Hunter, *Church for the Unchurched* (Nashville: Abingdon Press, 1996), 62-63.

4. Stan Toler and Alan Nelson, *The Five-Star Church* (Ventura, Calif.: Regal Books, 1999).

Chapter 2

1. *The Executive Speaker* 19:9 (September 1998), 8.

2. George Barna, *The Power of Vision* (Ventura, Calif.: Regal Books, 1992), 36.

3. George Barna, *Turning Vision into Action* (Ventura, Calif.: Regal Books, 1996), 36.

4. Ibid.

5. Mike Vance and Diane Deacon, *Break Out of the Box* (Franklin Lakes, N.J.: Career Press, 1996), 13.

6. Bert Nanus, *Visionary Leadership* (San Francisco: Jossey-Bass Publisher, 1992), 50.

7. John Maxwell, *Vision: The Process of Passing It On!* (Atlanta: IN-JOY, 1996), 17.

8. Vance and Deacon, *Break Out of the Box*, 29.

Chapter 3

1. Joke from Bob Newman, maintenance worker at Community Baptist Church.

2. From a Promise Keepers message delivered at War Memorial Stadium in Little Rock, Arkansas, by James Ryle, 1998.

3. RAM stands for random access memory and represents the amount of available memory to run a program. In this context, people have only so much available "think power" and often fill up this available space with the unimportant or urgent and miss out on what's being communicated to them.

Chapter 4

1. Steven Covey, *Seven Habits of Highly Effective People Tape Series*, recorded 1995 in Provo, Utah, and available from Franklin Covey Distributors.

Chapter 5

1. "Light Lines," *Net Results*, February 1990, 19.

2. Daryl R. Conner, *Managing at the Speed of Change* (New York: Villard Books, 1992), 92.

3. Jim Herrington, Mike Bonem, James H. Furr, *Leading Congregational Change* (San Francisco: Jossey-Bass, 2000), 35.

4. Ibid., 41.

5. Paraphrased from *Parables, Etc.* 18:8 (October 1998), 5.

6. Robert W. Bradford and J. Peter Duncan, *Simplified Strategic Planning* (Worcester, Mass.: Chandler House Press, 20000, 3.

7. Quoted in Raymond McHenry, *In Other Words* (Beaumont, Tex: McHenry Publishing, 1998), 67.

Chapter 6

1. Glenn Wagner and Glen Martin, *Your Pastor's Heart* (Chicago: Moody Press, 1998), 60.

2. Patrick Morley, *The Man in the Mirror* (Grand Rapids: Zondervan Publishing House, 1997.

3. Bruce Bugbee, Don Cousins, and Bill Hybels, *Network* (Grand Rapids: Zondervan Publishing House and Willow Creek Resources, 1994).

4. George Hunter, *How to Reach Secular People* (Nashville: Abingdon Press, 1995), 43-53.

5. Alan Nelson and Stan Toler, *The Five-Star Church* (Ventura, Calif.: Regal Books, 1999), 45.

Chapter 7

1. Glenn M. Parker, *Team Players and Teamwork* (San Francisco: Jossey-Bass Inc., Publishers, 1990).

2. Ibid., 9.

3. George Cladis, *Leading the Team-Based Church* (San Francisco: Jossey-Bass Publishers, 1999), ix.

4. Ibid. The majority of Cladis's book introduces the following models well worth the study of any leadership core: The Covenanting Team, the Visionary Team, the Culture-Creating Team, the Collaborative Team, the Trusting Team, the Empowering Team, and the Learning Team.

5. Bobb Biehl and Ted W. Engstrom, *Increasing Your Boardroom Confidence* (Phoenix: Questar Publishers, 1988), 54.

6. Jim Herrington, Mike Bonem, James H. Furr, *Leading Congregational Change* (San Francisco: Jossey-Bass, 2000), 128.

7. Perry M. Smith, *Rules and Tools for Leaders* (Garden City Park, N.Y.: Avery Publishing Group, 1998), 45.

8. Ibid., 69.

9. Morley, *The Man in the Mirror,* 54.

10. Stan Toler and Larry Gilbert, *The Pastor's Playbook* (Kansas City: Beacon Hill Press of Kansas City, 2000), 41.